A PECULIAR PROPHET

William H. Willimon
and the Art of Preaching

EDITED BY

MICHAEL A. TURNER

AND

WILLIAM F. MALAMBRI III

Abingdon Press
Nashville

A PECULIAR PROPHET
WILLIAM H. WILLIMON AND THE ART OF PREACHING

Copyright © 2004 by Abingdon Press

All rights reserved.

This book is printed on acid-free paper.

Library of Congress Cataloging-in-Publication Data

A peculiar prophet : William H. Willimon and the art of preaching / edited by
  Michael A. Turner and William F. Malambri III.
    p. cm.
  Includes bibliographical references and index.
  ISBN 0-687-00061-0 (binding: adhesive perfect : alk. paper)
  1. Willimon, William H. 2. Methodist Church—Sermons. 3. Preaching. I. Willimon,
William H. II. Turner, Michael A., 1975- III. Malambri III, William F., 1974-

  BX8333.W46P43 2004
  251'.0092—dc22

                                                                          2004009485

04 05 06 07 08 09 10 11 12 13—10 9 8 7 6 5 4 3 2 1

MANUFACTURED IN THE UNITED STATES OF AMERICA

CONTENTS

CHAPTER 1

WHY WILLIMON?

Michael A. Turner

Our Current Homiletical Milieu

At the beginning of the twenty-first century, the art of preaching is in peril. The problem is not that there are fewer preachers than at any other time in the life of the church—though many denominations are suffering from shortages of clergy. Rather, assaulted on all sides, preachers in this peculiar time lack sufficient theological resources and ecclesial practices to produce preaching worthy of the name.

Part of the problem is that modern Western culture is detrimental to the practice of preaching. Entertainment reigns. Having lost our desire to be saved, we want simply to be amused. Desperate to be "relevant" in what has been dubbed the MTV age, many preachers have sought to stay atop their games, *not* by digging in, doing serious study, opening the pages of the Early Church Fathers and Mothers, delving more deeply into scriptural exegesis, and becoming more theologically and biblically sound, but rather by latching onto the latest technological developments and gadgetry of the entertainment industry.[1]

Instead of carefully crafting sermons around the biblical text, many preachers have attempted to produce more "effective" sermons using movie clips and PowerPoint slideshows. That so many preachers have rushed to baptize the use of slideshows and movie clips in sermons only reveals a lack of faith in our God miraculously to produce the hearing that Christian preaching deserves. Moreover, as Neil Postman has shown in his seminal work, *Amusing Ourselves to Death,* technology is not neutral.[2] Because most movies mimic commercials, which are their cultural cousins, it is hard to separate the medium and the message. In fact, the medium transforms the message. Movies, other "relevant" media, and communication tactics are merely business endeavors dominated by a consumerist culture, and preaching that attempts to use these technologies finds it difficult to free itself from the grip of consumerism.[3]

Consumerism, like the entertainment culture, also threatens the art of preaching.[4] In fact, even more ubiquitous and insidious than our penchant for entertainment, is the ever-expanding, all-encompassing "market." More and more, the market seems to drive everything, including the practices of the Church and its pastors. When the rest of the world is geared toward "user-friendliness" and pleasing the consumer, the truth of the gospel can be bad business.

The "therapeutic," on the other hand, is good business. So much of preaching, when it is not driven by our desire for entertainment, is driven by the therapeutic culture in which we live. Bookstores sell self-help books by the thousands.[5] "Spirituality" is *en vogue*, and the deleterious result is preaching that calls us to no greater authority than that which is self-derived. Instead of providing a Word from the Outside, from the God perfectly revealed to us in the life, death, and resurrection of Jesus Christ, therapeutic preaching seeks to help Christians solve their own problems by getting them in touch with their so-called needs—needs that have never been critiqued in the light of the gospel to judge whether or not they

2

are needs worth having. In the end, the therapeutic is yet another way in which the market has its way with and *consumes* Christian preaching.[6]

However, the effects of the market do not stop there. If anything has a market these days, it is information. The Internet and other tools of information dissemination have placed at our fingertips far more information than can ever be digested or retained. That is good news for the preacher who legitimately desires to research and study. The Internet, however, can also open up a wilderness full of temptations.

Bereft of a strong sense of vocation and busy trying to be all things to all people, many pastors have found the Internet to be a shortcut to sermon preparation. Every day new Web sites pop up, offering to solve all clerical time management woes by rescuing pastors from the onus of sermon preparation. Given the proliferation of preaching crutches available on the Internet, it would not be surprising if even www.justtoolazytoprepare.com became a resounding success.

At their best, such Web sites offer some semblance of a community—albeit a virtual one—in which to engage in discourse about the preaching task and particular Scripture passages. However, at their worst, such sites have endangered the preaching ministry of the church in a number of ways, not the least of which has been to encourage plagiarism. Moreover, it is hard to imagine how a sermon written by someone in a completely different ecclesial context can truly engage a people for whom it was not designed. Without a doubt, trite, sappy, acontextual Internet sermons are no substitute for artful, engaging encounters with Scripture, encounters borne only through homiletical disciplines.

Just the other day, I received in the mail an advertisement for a sermon publication. "Too busy to write sermons? Let us do it for you. Sermons written by pastors for pastors." Not only encouraging plagiarism but also fostering intellectual laziness, the morality of such resources is not the morality of the Church.

However, because of the demise of imaginative preaching, some laypeople *prefer* prepackaged Internet homilies to the real thing. Not too long ago, I was discussing the sermonic sloth and plagiaristic tendencies of many pastors with a friend who is a Catholic layperson. His response: "I *wish* our priest would get his sermons off the Internet! At least *then* they would be tolerable, and I would know that he had done *some* preparation before stepping into the pulpit. Taking the time to print out a sermon is better than no preparation at all."

One can see his point. Internet theology warmed up and served again can be better than no theology at all. However, passing off another's work as one's own is nothing short of lying—sinning.[7] There is nothing wrong with a voracious reading appetite for sermons, novels, and short stories—in fact, those are good disciplines—but rampant plagiarism among the clergy is not only damaging to the laity, it is also deleterious to clergy character and imagination. Sadly, those most likely to fall to the temptation of Internet iniquity are the least likely to be reading these pages.[8]

Artful preaching takes time and intellectual labor. Imagination requires cultivation and hard work. To the world, the time required to cultivate imagination and prepare to preach may look like a waste. But, to borrow from Marva Dawn's description of worship, it is a *royal* waste.[9]

Given the current cultural and homiletical milieu, preachers who truly desire to be artisans face an ominous task. We need many things: vocational clarity, accountability, discipline, theological formation, and so forth. But perhaps that which is most needed by preachers today is role models, mentors.[10] Preachers are groping for master craftspersons who embody the virtues; who stand firm against the cultural currents of consumerism, entertainment, and the therapeutic; who take seriously the vocation to preach and do the necessary but difficult work to prepare their minds and souls to fulfill their vocation. Such craftspersons are needed to teach pastors the moves, gestures, and practices that produce Christian preaching worthy of the name.

Those seeking to be homiletical artisans must be willing to learn the craft by becoming apprentices to master craftspersons. Imitation is a great teacher. All preachers can point to those saints gone before who have influenced their proclamation. Great preachers are those who have been able to assimilate the virtues of those saints into their own preaching life. The great orator Martin Luther King Jr. even memorized entire sermons of great preachers. Then, he delivered them to mirrors and fellow homiletical students, mimicking the style, parroting the pacing, and perfecting the pronunciation and art of the preachers he admired.[11]

Amid today's preponderance of homiletical pitfalls, pastors who model theological discipline and rhetorical power are needed more than ever. The gestures of a good preacher include attention to and playful conversation with the biblical text, as well as the cultivation of a life of prayer and study. Although preachers of this caliber are in short supply, the editors of this book have been blessed to study under one such person. Looking over his shoulder, mimicking his moves, and incorporating some of his habits has made us better preachers. We have been blessed to study under Will Willimon.

William H. Willimon: A Master Craftsman

"Will Willimon has never had an unpublished thought!"[12] Though this claim is meant as a quip, there is always some truth in jest. Since his ordination in 1972, he has published an average of two books per year[13] as well as countless articles and editorials, and all of this work is *in addition* to preaching week in and week out.

The breadth and scope of his work is oceanic. The Academy of Parish Clergy proclaimed two of his books, *Worship as Pastoral Care* and *Pastor: The Theology and Practice of Ordained Ministry*, "most useful books for clergy" in the year that they were published, and over a million copies of his books have been sold. Yet, while he has dared to venture into many different spheres of life—worship,[14] history,[15] literary criticism,[16] church reform,[17] higher education reform,[18] governmental politics,[19] and life transitions[20]—first and foremost Willimon is a pastoral theologian[21] whose primary message is that the God revealed in Jesus matters for *everything* in life. Thus his most influential work has been in calling the Church to be a faithful witness to the God revealed to us in the person of Jesus Christ.

Writing extensively in the areas of Christology, ecclesiology, the Sacraments, and the various aspects of pastoral leadership, Will Willimon has sought to reform the Church by focusing on the formation of disciples in the particularity of the faith. By the artful use of language, stinging wit, and an eye for the ironies of life, Willimon has helped form two generations of Christians—lay and clergy alike—in the peculiar, countercultural ways of the Christian faith. Constantly in conversation with those who have lived the faith before us,[22] Willimon is content to live in the vast mystery of the faith, seeking neither the easy answers of fundamental Christianity nor the warm, fuzzy theological vacuum of Protestant liberalism. Carefully toeing the line of historical Christianity, Willimon seems peculiar to many Christians captured in modernity.

Not only has Willimon written extensively, but also the world has paid attention. A recent article published in the *Christian Century* shows that Willimon is among the most widely read authors in the Church. In "Pastors' Picks: What Preachers are Reading,"[23] Jackson Carroll shares the results of a survey aimed at discovering the reading habits of pastors. Among the authors most read by mainline Protestants, Willimon was second only to Henri J. M. Nouwen. When Willimon speaks, pastors listen.

Poignant Preaching

While his books have been widely consumed and many people have benefited from them, many believe that Willimon's most important contribution to the Church lies in his preaching. For this reason, while we shall have occasion to refer to Willimon's published work at different points throughout this book, our primary focus will be on him as a representative, influential, and formative preacher of our age.

For thirty years this pulpiteer has scarcely missed a Sunday preaching at one place or another, including weekday preaching at hundreds of pastors' schools and college campuses. It is in his preaching that his theological insights, born of the biblical narrative, have assaulted and transformed the lives of nascent and mature Christians alike. Evidence of the public appreciation for his preaching lies in Baylor University's naming Will as one of the twelve most effective preachers in the English-speaking world.

In a world that believes that talk is cheap and actions speak louder than words, Will Willimon dares to believe that the God who created the world by speaking into the formless void intends to redeem the world through the power of the Word. Words, according to Willimon, are not empty. Instead, words continue to create worlds, to construct realities. As an ordained Christian clergyperson, it has been his task for over thirty years to master the world of words in order that through them he may more perfectly proclaim *the* Word. In the end, he contends with Saint Augustine that preachers are merely "merchants of words." Words are all preachers have to work with.[24]

And yet, Willimon knows, perhaps better than most, that if the words of the preacher are not rooted in *the* Word, then the result is fruitless drivel—preaching that deserves some adjective other than *Christian*. Christian preaching is about God: Father, Son, and Holy Spirit. "Preaching 'works' because this God intends to speak, to make contact with a beloved, still being redeemed creation."[25] The God revealed in Jesus is incredibly intrusive, relentless to have an audience and capture us as God's own. That reality gives life to the words of the preacher.

Penchant for Particularity

Many pastors these days are into an apologetics that tries to make the Christian faith more palatable to its "cultured despisers." In a culture of consumer capitalism and "church shopping," apologetics is too easily reduced to the attempt to make the gospel more marketable by universalizing it—de-emphasizing the particularities of the faith. The result of such a snare is the notion that Christians believe pretty much what any rational, red-blooded American person would believe if given the chance to think clearly enough. The driving force behind such an effort is the attempt to make people act or seem Christian without conversion, without the transformation of the Holy Spirit made possible by the person and work of Jesus Christ.

Will Willimon is not into apologetics. Knowing that repentance, conversion, and transformation are an integral part of following Jesus, he does not try to "translate" the gospel into something any "rational"[26] person can understand. In other words, Willimon knows that the gospel will never "make sense" to anyone without that person stepping in line behind Jesus and submitting to the transforming grace of God.[27] Armed with that knowledge, he lifts up the particularity of the faith—a particularity based in the Second Person of the Trinity.

Dorothy Day popularized a saying she originally heard from Cardinal Suhard.[28] The task of the Christian is to be "a living mystery. [This] means to live in such a way that one's life would not make sense if God did not exist."[29] Willimon seeks to apply that same conviction to his preaching: The task of Christian preaching is to preach in such a way that one's proclamation would not make sense if God did not exist.

We must learn to preach again in such a way as to demonstrate that if there is no Holy Spirit, if Jesus has not been raised from the dead, then our preaching is doomed to fall upon deaf ears. Our preaching ought to be so confrontive, so in violation of all that contemporary Americans think they know, that it requires no less than a miracle to be heard. We preach best with a reckless confidence in the power of the gospel to evoke the audience it deserves.[30]

Convinced that the Bible is interesting and that the gospel is engaging, Willimon has been content to trust his material. Over many years, he has honed his perception to *highlight* the idiosyncratic, challenging, and weird aspects of Scripture—not apologize for them. Identifying the intensely particular ways of Jesus, he then brings the oddity of the Church's story into dramatic collision with our preconceived notions and governing presuppositions. Willimon, it seems, never tires of telling the Church just how distinctive our way of life should be because of the particular God who has captured us.

One of the regular worshipers at Duke Chapel jokingly contends that, in reality, Willimon has only three sermons which he preaches with endless repetition: (1) "God is large, mysterious, and there is no way I could explain it to someone like you," (2) "Life is a mess, and there is no way that I could explain it to someone like you," and (3) "Christianity is weird, odd, peculiar; I can't believe you people actually want to be Christians."

These are indeed themes that run through much of Willimon's preaching as he seeks to allow God to speak. Yet, even if these were the only sermons Willimon ever preached, they are definitely sermons twenty-first-century Americans need to hear. First, narcissistic people need to be reminded that God *is* large and mysterious. The theological nature of Willimon's preaching has good precedent: The Bible speaks first and foremost about God before it ever speaks about us. Second, in a culture of self-reliance and "independence" we need to be reminded that life *is* a mess. Our sin and fallenness render us incapable of saving ourselves, which takes us back to point number one. It's all about God, not us. Finally, in a time when many Christians are apologetic and seek to blend into the crowd, we need to be reminded that Christianity *is* peculiar, weird, odd. Willimon has a penchant for doing just that.

A Parting Word and How to Use This Book

With equal parts creativity and courage, Will has dared to emphasize what is distinctive about the Christian gospel. This theological derring-do has won him admirers as well as detractors. However, there is no doubt that Will Willimon has exercised a tremendous influence over his students—of which Will Malambri and I are two. Like good apprentices, we have sought to emulate his creativity, craft, and theological seriousness. To some extent, it seems to have worked. In order that we might hold each other accountable to taking our preaching task seriously, we e-mail our sermons back and forth to each other, and often one or the other of us will comment, "That sounds very Willimonian." *Most* of the time, that is a compliment.

By collecting some of Willimon's sermons and arranging them according to four overriding themes of his life and work, we hope that this volume will provide an opportunity for others to apprentice themselves to this peculiar prophet of God's Word. Imitating a master craftsperson cannot help but add tools to the preacher's kit and make him or her a better preacher.[31]

Yet, blind imitation of even the most carefully chosen mentors is ill advised. Apprentices learn from the weaknesses as well as the strengths of those with whom they study. For this reason, it is very important to *practice* preaching instead of merely gaining pulpit experience. Too often preachers mistake experience in preaching with its practice. "An experienced, mature preacher is one who has had lots of Sundays to fail."[32] To *practice* preaching rightly means submitting to critique, to honest evaluation about the faithfulness of proclaimed Word to its source, the written Word.[33]

For this reason, we have asked several other homiletical masters and theologians to respond to Will's sermons. Through their critique and the conversation it engenders, the reader will be made privy to the insights of some of the most sought-after preachers and theologians in the world. Taking care to evaluate these insights and minding the moves of the master they critique will put you well on your way to becoming a master yourself.

Attending to the insights and craft of master craftspersons will go a long way toward shaping the reader in the homiletical craft; however, artful, faithful preaching requires more than good mentors. Discipline, faith, and much prayer are prerequisites to good preaching. Disciplined Scripture reading is necessary since the source of good preaching is the biblical text. Playful, imaginative, daily encounters with Scripture provide the fuel for proclamation and keep the fires of creativity stoked. Merely reading Scripture, however, is useless unless the preacher has faith to believe that the wild claims of the gospel are true. Our job as preachers is not to explain away the Scriptures, but to boldly proclaim them. That requires faith. Finally, only the Holy Spirit vivifies Christian preaching. A fervent prayer life is the channel through which the life-giving Spirit flows into our proclamation and provides indescribable joy for the preacher as he or she begins to see the transformation wrought in the Church and world through faithful preaching.

However, not even good mentors, discipline, faith, and prayer are enough to guarantee that our preaching will be "effective." Willimon would be the first to tell us that all our homiletical failures as preachers may not be due to our sermonic ineptitude.[34] Some of our failures can be attributed only to Jesus himself. Preaching the gospel of Jesus is not always good news to some— particularly to wealthy, comfortable, "self-sufficient" congregations who like "to make up their own minds." There is risk involved in proclaiming truth. Daring to preach the truth may not make you a "success." But, as theologian John Howard Yoder reminds us, we are not called to "effectiveness" or even "success," but rather to faithfulness.[35] It is our prayer that this volume will provide a window into the preaching practices of one peculiar prophet whom we deem faithful, as well as grant new perspective into the craft of preaching. In the process, we hope that you, the reader, grow in faithfulness as a preacher.

In addition, we hope that this volume will honor one who is not only our mentor, but also our friend. Good apprentices mind the moves of those under whom they work, but good master craftspersons take their apprentices under their wing, encourage, correct, and befriend their apprentices. Will Willimon has done just that for us and many more like us.

By the time this book goes to print, Will will have been teaching at Duke Divinity School for twenty years. On behalf of all his apprentices in that stretch of time, I say to him, "Thank you." Keep challenging, critiquing, encouraging, and correcting.

P A R T   I

THEMES IN WILLIMON'S LIFE AND WORK

CHAPTER 2

THEOLOGICAL PREACHING:
"IT'S ABOUT GOD, NOT YOU"

Easter as an Earthquake

MATTHEW 28:1-10

Easter, 1999

Suddenly there was a great earthquake; for an angel of the Lord, descending from heaven, came and rolled back the stone and sat on it. (Matthew 28:2)

John says that they get to the tomb on Easter morning, and it's empty. Then, they go back home.

Go back home? Reminds you of the two disciples in Luke on the way to Emmaus. "Some women told us that Jesus had been raised from the dead, but we had already planned to have supper over in Emmaus. We couldn't change our reservations."

A man is raised from the dead and you can't cancel lunch? How dumb are these disciples?

So my friend Stanley Hauerwas, in dialogue with Marcus Borg of the errant Jesus Seminar, says, "Marcus thinks the disciples had an experience. They said, 'Wasn't it great being with Jesus before they killed him? You remember those great stories he told? The lectures, er, *sermons?* Just thinking about it makes him seem almost still here. Yep, by God, he *is* still here. Let's all close our eyes and believe real hard that he's still here. Okay?'"

Hey, Jesus Seminar, the disciples weren't that creative! These were not imaginative minds we're dealing with here. They were the sort of people who could see an empty tomb and not let it spoil lunch. You don't get an idea like the bodily resurrection of Jesus out of people with brains like Simon Peter's.

In short, *the disciples were people like us.*

People like us are the sort of folk who like to believe that you can have resurrection and still have the world as it was yesterday. We want to have Easter and still have our world unrocked by resurrection. We are amazingly well adjusted to the same old world.

I think that's why Matthew says that, when there was Easter, the whole earth shook. Luke does Easter as a meal on Sunday evening with the Risen Christ. John has resurrected Jesus encounter Mary Magdalene in the garden. But Matthew? Easter is an earthquake with doors shaken off tombs and dead people walking the streets, the stone rolled away by the ruckus and an impudent angel sitting on it.

I've been in an earthquake, even though I'm not from L.A. I was preaching in Alaska, and during my sermon, the earth heaved a moment that seemed forever. The little church shook. The Alaskan Methodists sat there like it was another day at the office. The only response came from the woman who said, "How about that, the light fixtures didn't fall this time." I ended my sermon immediately. I was shaken by the earthquake, but also a bit shaken by those nonchalant Alaskans. Afterward (at lunch!) I asked the pastor, "What the heck would it take to get this congregation's attention? I'd hate to have to preach to them every Sunday!"

Matthew says Easter is an earthquake that shook the whole world.

We modern types try to "explain" the resurrection. One says that Jesus was in a deep, drugged coma and woke up. Another said that the disciples got all worked up in their grief and just fantasized the whole thing.

You can't "explain" a resurrection. *Resurrection explains us.* The truth of Jesus tells on the faces of the befuddled disciples who witnessed it. Not one of them expected, wanted Easter. Death, defeat, while regrettable, are utterly explainable.

"It was a good campaign while it lasted. But we didn't get him elected Messiah. Death has the last word. We had hoped, but you've got to face facts. You want some lunch?"

The world is in the tight death-grip of the "facts." All that lives, dies. The good get it in the end. Face facts. It may be a rather somber world, but it is *our* world where things stay tied down and what dies stays that way. And there are few surprises. This is us.

But Easter is about God. It is not about the resuscitation of a dead body. That's resuscitation, not resurrection. It's not about the "immortality of the soul," some divine spark that endures after the end. That's Plato, not Jesus. It's about God, not God as an empathetic but ineffective good friend, or some inner experience, but a God who creates a way when there is no way, a God who makes war on evil until evil is undone, a God who raises dead Jesus just to show us who's in charge here.

I don't know this for sure, but I think that the Easter earthquake angel perched on the rock rolled from the tomb was the same angel who, back in Matthew 1 (vv. 8-25), shook Joseph awake one night with the news that his fiancée was pregnant. (Talk about an earthquake!) See my point? God did on Easter in invading the tomb what God did on Christmas in a virgin's womb. Made a way when there was no way. Took charge. The same angel who was sent to tell Joseph, "Name the baby, Emmanuel, God with us," was the angel who told the women, "Don't be afraid. He isn't here. He's been raised." Little "God with us" grew up, got crucified, made the earth shake, and is on the move to take back the world.

On the cross, the world did all it could to Jesus. At Easter, God did all God could to the world. And the earth shook.

You don't explain that. You witness it. That's why the Risen Christ appeared first to his own disciples. They had heard him teach, seen him heal, watched as he loved the poor and attacked the rich, watched him be arrested by the soldiers, tried by the judge, and crucified.

Why would Jesus come back first to his disciples? Because they were the ones able to recognize that this Risen Lord was none other than the Crucified Jesus. Crucifixion wasn't just an unfortunate mistake in the Roman legal system, the first-century Judean equivalent of the O. J. Simpson fiasco. Crucifixion was the inevitable, predictable result of saying the things Jesus said, and doing the things Jesus did, and being the Savior Jesus was. This is what the world always does to people who threaten the world. Face facts.

But on Easter God inserted a new fact. God took the cruel cross and made it the means of triumph. God—the same Creator who made light from darkness, a world from void—God took the worst we could do, all our death-dealing doings, and led them out toward life. And the earth shook.

A new world was thereby offered to us. Jesus came back to forgive the very disciples who had forsaken him. The world is about forgiveness, as it turns out, not vengeance. And the earth shook.

Jesus picked up a piece of bread and ate it, and you could see the nail prints in his hands. The world is about life, as it turns out, not death. And the earth shook.

In the fifties, in China, there was a devastating earthquake. But as a result of the quake, a huge boulder was dislodged from a mountain, thus exposing a great cache of wonderful artifacts from a thousand years ago. A new world suddenly became visible.

When the stone was rolled away and the earth shook, we got our first glimpse of a new world, a world where death doesn't have the last word, a world where injustice is made right and innocent suffering is vindicated by the intrusion of a powerful God.

The women came out to the cemetery to write one more chapter in the long, sad story of death's ascendancy, one more episode of how the good always get it in the end. This is the way the world ends, not with a bang but a whimper of resignation at death's dark victory.

And then, the earth heaved, an angel appeared, the stone was rolled away, Caesar's soldiers shook. The angel plopped himself down on the stone in one final act of impudent defiance of death, and the soldiers, and all that, and said to the women, "*Don't be afraid*. You're looking for Jesus? He isn't here."

Then that angel turned to the soldiers and said, "*Be* afraid. Everything your world is built on is being shaken."

Nobody went back the same way they came.

Thy Kingdom Come,
on Earth as in Heaven

JOHN 20:1-18

April 15, 2001

"Death is no longer a downer," proclaimed *USA Today*.[1] "Death's former finality has been upstaged by a new vision of the afterlife in which the dearly departed can communicate with their loved ones, influence events, even come back to the mortal world for another go-round."

We've always liked movies that end "happily ever after." In today's pop culture, happiness "ever after" has been extended. One of the most popular TV shows, *Buffy the Vampire Slayer*, features Buffy and her boyfriend, Angel, who just won't die. Then there was *Meet Joe Black*, an interminable movie about the delayed termination of a tycoon. In *What Dreams May Come*, Robin Williams is killed in a car crash but is incredibly reunited with the family dog in a sort of German romantic landscape. "The message is that love can survive death, that our mortality doesn't doom us," says scriptwriter Ron Bass.

Titanic has Jack and Rose happy after all, despite Jack's drowning, reunited on the grand staircase as if the whole iceberg thing was a joke.

Gerald Celente (author of *Trends 2000*) theorizes that we Baby Boomers are watching parents die, getting AIDS, saying to ourselves, "Wait a minute, a generation as wonderful as ours can't die; maybe we won't."

When Meryl Streep dared to die of cancer in *One True Thing*, it was a box office bomb, giving credence to James Swanson's idea (in the *Chicago Tribune*) of "the grandiose narcissism and impertinence of Boomers. They're determined that, for them, death will be different." He calls it "Faith Lite." Princess Di is Elton John's "candle in the wind" that goes on forever. See? We just go on and on—immortal, like *Jack Frost*'s Michael Keaton in which a deceased father comes back as his son's snowman. Give me a break!

Just one thing about all this immortality glitz: *None of it has anything to do with Easter.*

You heard the story. *Jesus really died.* He did not appear to die, was not asleep. He died a death more cruel than can be conceived. He wasn't dead for a moment on the operating room table having an out-of-body experience; he was sealed in the grave for three days. The disciples did not deceive themselves about his death, think that, though crucified, "he will live on in our memories," or any such pagan drivel.

Did you hear how the disciples got to the first Easter? *In great grief.* They came to Jesus' tomb with no cheap, false consolation: "his message will never die," or "if we endow a chair at the university, no one will ever forget him." When they saw the empty tomb, they didn't think, "Jesus is immortal." They thought, "Somebody stole his body." There's a lot of weeping and real grief in the story as John tells it. Tears are the appropriate response to the reality, the finality, and the totality of death.

Yet, within days, Jesus' followers began to understand that what had happened to Jesus was "according to the Scriptures." Israel believed that one day God was going to solve the problem of Israel's suffering and oppression and, while God was at it, God would solve the problem of evil, injustice, death in all the world. The Scriptures promised a day of divine victory, and on Easter the disciples discovered that day in the resurrection of Jesus. The cross, which they had thought was the end of their relationship with Jesus, was really the beginning. Easter was God's answer to the question: What shall be done about the world?

In *The Green Mile*, when something weird, good, and spiritual is about to happen, this odd glitter began falling from the sky, things got all fuzzy, and blue, and strange. That's the way Hollywood does God. God is something otherworldly, weird, fuzzy. Well, note that John goes to some length to demonstrate that what happened to Jesus on Easter, while unexpected and strange, happened *here, now*. It was "still dark," the "linen cloth" is rolled carefully. Mary weeps. A man appears; she thinks him a gardener. These are mundane details from daily life, where people weep and are confused, and things end in tragedy—details from daily death.

It's resurrection, *not* immortality of the soul, not even "life after death." There *is* life after death, and God's people can expect it. But it won't be Hollywood's "life after death." Christians don't believe in the immortality of a disembodied soul. We believe, as we say in the Creed, in "the *resurrection* of the body." Not the *resuscitation* of the body, a corpse come back to life. That happens almost daily at Duke Hospital. It's not the immortality of the soul, some divine spark that goes on living despite our death. That happens only in Hollywood. We believe that dead Jesus was raised by a loving God whose loving power would not be defeated by death, here, now.

The disciples found the grave empty. Jesus' dead body wasn't there. When the Risen Christ appeared to Mary, he appeared not as some disembodied ghost, a spirit, but in his body. To be sure, it was some sort of changed body, for she did not recognize him until he spoke. But it was his body. Later the Risen Christ would eat with his disciples, be touched by them in his resurrected body.

So we Christians believe, as they say, "When you're dead, you're dead." Death really is death, *finis*. But we also believe that, in resurrection, God decisively acted, defeated death, making a way when we thought no way, here, now.

This is better than Hollywood. The resurrection of the body, Jesus' or yours, means that this world matters, now. We may not know exactly how our resurrected bodies will look. As John says, "it does not yet appear what we shall be" (1 John 3:2 [RSV]). But we do believe that just as Jesus' body was raised by the love of God, so shall ours.

This means that this world matters. The matter of this world matters. We're not bound for some disembodied spiritual never-never-land. God has made a decisive bridgehead against the onslaught of death here, now. There is no present pain that is not transformed in Christ's resurrection.

That's why we pray each Sunday, "Thy kingdom come, *on earth as it is in heaven.*" Resurrection is about God getting at last what God wants here, now, on earth, in the body, that which God will one day have in heaven.

It's not just that there's a cushy afterlife in store for some of us who make the grade, someday. As N. T. Wright says, if it were, then Christianity could be justly accused of being pie-in-the-sky-by-and-by religion rather than the thy-kingdom-come-on-earth-as-in-heaven religion that it is. If Easter is just Jesus exiting the tomb in some ethereal spiritual sense, leaving a body in the tomb to rot, leaving the world to stew in its own juice, where is the hope? Better go make movies that do death as only apparent, and spirits taking off for pastel skies. Resurrection is more than a warm feeling, some vague spiritual inclination. It's about king-dom-on-earth-as-in-heaven, a new heaven and new earth first hinted at in the resurrection of the body of Jesus on Easter, one day to come in fullness when God does Easter in full for the whole of creation. God faced evil and death on Good Friday, then on Easter, triumphed. Now God intends to do for the whole world, through us Easter people, what was done for Jesus on Easter.

In Hollywood, when people die, everything tends to get fuzzy, vaporous, pink. Here in church, we do Easter with the things of this world—candles, flowers, parades, banners, and, above all, music. It's like a world out of tune, a world marching to the dirge-like beat of death, finally gets back its intended tune, as if the whole creation, once destined for futility and death, now soars in song, healed, reclaimed by a God determined not to leave us to death.

Karl Marx charged that Christianity lulls people into political complacency because Christianity has got nothing but heaven in its head, some future spiritual experience removed from the here and the now. "John Brown's body lies amoldering in the grave, but God goes marching on!"

No. The first witnesses to Easter knew *something* had happened. Their world had been entered, encountered, transformed, rocked, reformed. Easter wasn't God saying, "Let me get you out of this deadly, tearful world." Easter was God saying, "Let me show you what I am doing to you and your world, here, now."

Take away the resurrection of the body, and Marx is right. Christianity is mere wish fulfillment, escape into some nirvana of our creation, escape from problems of the here and the now.

Take the resurrection of the body seriously—or to the point of our music, *joyously*—and you have a great responsibility laid upon you. If you can sing, "Alleluia! Christ is risen," you are saying that Jesus Christ really is Lord and all other would-be lords of this world are not. When we sing, "The strife is o'er, the battle won," it means that we must join in the mopping-up actions wherever evil still dares to challenge the reign of a good and loving God.

The Jesus Seminar of a few years ago said that, at Easter, what happened was that the disciples of Jesus had an experience of Christ's presence.

No. That won't lift the luggage. The resurrection wasn't inner, spiritual experience. It was God's act in Jesus Christ, the bodily, visible rising of a sun whose glory puts all other suns to shame. Today the master of defeat and death has been defeated. So Paul says that, in the resurrection of Jesus, every ruler, every pompous politician and presumptive power, is being destroyed, "For he must reign until he has put all his enemies under his feet. The last enemy to be destroyed is death" (1 Corinthians 15:25-26). Easter is a great battle fought and won. And the kingdoms of this world shall be the kingdoms of our Christ, and he shall rule forever and ever. Amen!

(I have been helped in this sermon by N.T. Wright's "Grave Matters," a summary of some of his other works on the subject of resurrection, which appeared in Christianity Today, *April 6, 1998, pp. 51-53.)*

"It's About God, Not You!"

Fleming Rutledge

Rising to address a large gathering of Episcopalians at the Kanuga Conference Center in 1990, Will Willimon responded to the person who had just given him an introduction by saying, "Only an Anglican could manage to sound both gracious and condescending at the same time." This sally brought down the house. It would not have worked in another setting; the audience, being 100 percent Anglican, greatly enjoyed not only the joke on themselves but also the sly, knowing tone in which the riposte was delivered. This ability to match wit to context is a clue to Dr. Willimon's special gifts.

I was present on that occasion. It was the only time I have ever heard Willimon speak. During my ministry in New York our paths did not cross, and when I have preached at Duke University Chapel, he has quite naturally been preaching somewhere else. My relationship to him, therefore, is different from that of others; I have been neither student, protégé, parishioner, nor colleague. Yet I count myself high on the list of those who thank God for him, counting him among the most important influences in the world of preaching today—and that means *world*, not just the English-speaking world. It has meant so much that he has been out there breaking trail for the rest of us.

First, a note of personal gratitude. When I, an unknown preacher who had never even been in charge of a congregation, was preparing to publish my first book of sermons, Will Willimon consented to read my manuscript and write an introduction. It was an act of extraordinary generosity, and I believe that his lending his name and support in this way was largely responsible for lifting me from relative obscurity to a place in the wider Church. In my experience, there is just as much petty rivalry, jealousy, and withholding among the clergy as there is anywhere else—perhaps more—and this gift of a towering figure to an upstart still stands for me as an example of Christian magnanimity.

Moreover, this generous action on the part of Dr. Willimon was an example of his capacity, all too rare in these highly politicized times in the Church, to see nuance in the work of others. We are seeing American Christianity increasingly polarized between left and right, liberal and conservative, progressive and reactionary (whatever those stereotypical terms are construed to mean). Church leaders, lay and clergy alike, are labeled and shelved according to these superficial designations. Sometimes a single utterance on a hot topic like abortion, homosexuality, or feminist theology can doom a person to the margins of a mainline denomination. No matter what a person may say or think about poverty, the death penalty, exploitation of migrant workers, environmental depredation, racial prejudice, globalization, violence, or war, he or she is relentlessly judged by inflexible standards on hot-button issues like inclusive language, same-sex marriage, and various peace and justice issues. Willimon, however, while working squarely in the center of the mainline, has a capacity for discerning cant and revealing theological truth wherever he finds it. During the first Iraq war he received a note from a student at a conservative evangelical seminary who asked if Willimon could shed any light on a matter that perplexed him: Why, he asked, were "Bible-believing, evangelical" Christians in the USA supporting the war instead of preaching Christ to the millions of Iraqis who have never heard the gospel? With a reference to Billy Graham, who was at that time "cozying up to the president [George H. W. Bush]," Willimon agreed with his young correspondent that American Christians had "exchanged our story for Caesar's and thereby forfeited our ability to preach the gospel in Iraq." He concluded, "God send us more conservative, Bible-believing Christians!"[2] This is not a sentiment often heard in the mainlines.

This sets the stage for the first of four characteristics of Willimon's preaching that I want to identify.

His Sermons Are Fearless

Over a period of some decades Willimon has shown himself to be a fearless preacher. This is not to say that he is reckless, thoughtless, or heedless. Nor do I mean to suggest that he is never apprehensive, or that he is immune to the usual mortal foibles. I am using the word *fearless* in a strictly *theological* sense; he who fears God need fear no human being.[3] He is so secure in the power of the gospel that he feels no need to be measuring himself constantly against the latest politically acceptable position. When Willimon is verbally assaulted at the church door by an angry parishioner, he is surprised to find himself thinking, "I don't really care that you were upset by the sermon."[4] He knows that "offense and wounded sensibilities come with the territory."[5] Theologian Christopher L. Morse, like Willimon a Southerner and a Methodist, argues in his book *Not Every Spirit* that the early Christians were persecuted not for what they believed (*Kurios Iesous*—Jesus is Lord) but what they refused to believe (*Kurios Kaisar*—Caesar is Lord).[6] Morse argues that it is the task of a faithful theologian to identify those things that a Christian must refuse to believe.

This means also that the preacher must be willing to interpret passages dealing with God's judgment. Here is an illustration. A sermon on the Lukan Beatitudes called "Being Blessed and Cursed by Jesus" (not in this volume) has much less humor than most of Willimon's sermons. It depends for its force on three features: the shock of hearing Jesus say "damn you" to the rich and self-satisfied; the vivid evocation of the poor whom God favors;

and the three stories at the end that memorably illustrate "Blessed are you who are poor . . . who weep . . . who are hated and excluded on Christ's account." Then, in characteristic fashion, Willimon comes to an abrupt stop. He concludes by quoting one of his mentors, Carlyle Marney, who said to a group of clergy, "The trouble with you guys is not what you manage to affirm but what you fail to reject. You pleasing little preachers are always saying 'bless, bless, bless' when you ought to be saying 'damn, damn, damn.'" Imagine ending a sermon that way! Yet the attentive listener will have understood that this ending does not really recommend that preachers damn their congregations. The sermon is not at all an example of what is often derisively called "hellfire and damnation." Those who had ears to hear that day, February 11, 2001, must have known that Willimon was making a different point, because his three illustrations showed three people who had made painful but heroically right decisions to stand not only *for* something but also *against* something (casino gambling, the condition of homeless people, and a conspiracy to cover up wrongdoing). These are clearly admirable stances and worthy of emulation, so it is clear to the hearers that the emphasis is not on God's judgment of *people*, but *behavior*—greed and sloth, callousness and apathy, lies and deceit. As usual with Willimon, there is no hint of exhortation—that fatal error in so many sermons. Rather, Willimon offers descriptions and illustrations, each of them suited to Jesus' unique style of teaching by revelatory, not hortatory, means (the kingdom of God is like . . .).

Fearlessness in proclamation is essential for great preaching. Willimon understands himself as embattled and the Church as embattled. Christians must operate in the midst of alien territory. This stance is deeply, um, "embedded" in the New Testament, which is filled with battle imagery. As a fighter in the midst of the enemy's territory, Willimon has refused to collaborate or retreat. His pugnacity is suited to the situation that biblical preachers find themselves in. He tells a story about a United Methodist minister who attended a meeting with "a renowned contemporary interpreter of the Christian faith, a member of the Jesus Seminar [obviously Marcus Borg], and reported to a colleague,

'He is one of the nicest people in the world. Very open, irenic, and collegial in his conversation.' His colleague replied, 'Of course he is. Liberals are always open, irenic, and affirming. Why shouldn't they be? They've won!'"[7]

In his letters to the Galatians and the Corinthians, Paul the apostle engages in polemic because (speaking penultimately) he is about to lose. Willimon's sermons and writings are often polemical in this sense. God has given him an important beachhead to secure, and he will do it with the audacity and determination that the Spirit gives. His leadership from the pulpit is by necessity subversive and discomfiting—as unnerving as a guerrilla attack. He conducts lightning raids on the culture from his position behind enemy lines like Gideon against the Midianites. He is driven by the conviction that his commission from God requires this of him, even though—no, precisely *because*—our self-destructing culture is threatening to overwhelm the Church without the Church even noticing. Willimon knows that God's means of resistance is the faithful service of his commando units within the Church. Leading these forays is this preacher's God-given vocation, as it has been the vocation of the prophets and apostles before him. "This whole call thing is God's idea, from the first," he says in a sermon about Jeremiah:

> Leadership begins in the mind of God . . . the roots of biblical leadership are theological rather than anthropological. God's choice tells us more about the quality of God than the positive qualities of the people who are called to lead. . . . They are almost universally, laughably, *the wrong people*. . . . Maybe God likes a challenge. Maybe God, being a creator who makes something out of nothing, considers vocation a continuing aspect of creation.[8]

Because Willimon is secure in his vocation, or rather in the grasp of the One who calls in the first place (*vocare*, to call), he is able to strike out polemically at targets that others have deemed sacred. Out of the sermons I recently read, I made a list of some of the hits:

- children's sermons

- clergy as "change agents"

- "positive thinking"

- the "triumph of the human spirit"

- warm, fuzzy "spiritual" movies and TV shows

- the Jesus Seminar

- the supposed immortality of the soul

- "bureaucratic toadies"

- lotteries and casino gambling

- so-called "tolerance"

- self-help books and techniques

- "spirituality" in many of its guises

- Robert Schuller's preaching of "Be Happy Attitudes" and "Self-Esteem"

- near-death experiences as proof of the resurrection

- "faith in a vague God who neither speaks nor acts"

And most of all, perhaps, those who think the Church should retire its own language in favor of the language of our nationalistic, market-driven society.

This list of targets brings me to the second point about Willimon's work.

His Sermons Are Theological

Penetrating behind the assertion that fearlessness is necessary for truthful proclamation of the gospel, we come up with the title of this essay—"It's About God, Not Us." Here is Willimon's most fundamental contribution to the craft of preaching. His eye is on God. We can therefore say that his preaching is *theological*, rather than anthropological. This makes him stand out in a Church that often capitulates to the culture by allowing it to set the agenda, prescribe the correct responses, and provide the terminology. God (*theos*) has largely been banished to the sidelines. I hear a great many sermons around the country—unlike Willimon I am in the pulpit only one Sunday out of four—and I am astonished by the number of sermons I hear in which God is scarcely mentioned at all, and almost never as the subject of any verb except, sometimes, "love" (as in "God loves everybody"). To be sure, according to God's revelation of himself, *love* is entirely defined by God in Jesus Christ—but the love of God cannot adequately be conveyed independently of the *story* of God, which involves placing God at the head of many sentences as the subject of many powerful verbs. As we have suggested already, for instance, Willimon does not hesitate to pass along the news that God *judges* us, even though the designers of the lectionary have attempted to conceal this fact; and in many sermons he illustrates how God's judgment on us is an essential aspect of his love for us.

One of Willimon's emblematic sentences is, "Who is *the God who inserts himself* into history through Mary and Joseph?"[9] In such a sentence the offense of the proclamation is preserved—its particularity, its aggressiveness, its effrontery. We cannot speak of the biblical God without using verbs that sometimes offend. Willimon proclaims the God who "assaults" and "invades." He uses words like *subversive* and *pushy* and *uppity* to describe New Testament preaching. He speaks of God "seizing," and "commandeering" his servants. All of this vocabulary comes from God's own unexpurgated self-revelation. Over the years Willimon has given himself up to the Word of God in Scripture as the Word has more and more taken over his way of thinking. He is a man possessed, and that has always been a hallmark of truly great preaching.

Willimon wrote a blurb for Charles Bartow's book *God's Human Speech* in which he said that Bartow had not only written well about the language of preaching but also, and "perhaps best of all, he writes and thinks from *a clear theological position that is never out of view.*"[10] Willimon might as well have been writing about himself. Some of Bartow's words surely describe Willimon's own convictions; for example, "All the while we are making use of Scripture God also is making use of it, and has made use of it, and that use is not only relevant to but determinative for our use."[11] God has made use of his messenger, is shaping his messenger, is conforming his messenger to his Word. This certainty guides Willimon's entire body of work. It's about God, not about him—that is "the clear theological position that is never out of view."

This is crucial for at least two reasons. First, because many stellar preachers of Willimon's stripe have big egos, this conscious submission to the leading of God defines the difference between rampant self-aggrandizement and disciplined service. Second, and even more important, many preachers today have no clear theological position at all, perhaps because they have not been taught in any kind of systematic way. The curriculum in the seminaries has been disordered, confused, and fragmented in recent decades, as Willimon and Hauerwas have been saying for a long time. It is likely that many casual hearers (or readers) of Willimon's sermons do not notice the consistency of his theological position at first because the humor and the stories are so memorable, but no one preaching today is more grounded in the biblical faith. His sermons cohere because God is working through those decades of faithful reflection on the canon of Scripture to shape a mind that fears him alone. Paul refers to this Spirit-given combination of humility and fearlessness in 1 Corinthians 2:16: " 'Who has known the mind of the Lord so as to instruct him?' But we have the mind of Christ."

His Sermons Are Thoughtful

This reference to the mind of Christ brings me to a third characteristic of Willimon's preaching that I want to note. His sermons are the product of *thought*. Willimon is a thinker. You can
sense him thinking. You know he is thinking all the time. I am
not saying that he is a particularly systematic or disciplined
thinker, but it is obvious throughout his sermons and writings
that he has never ceased to read widely and reflect on what he
reads. My experience is that people who have uncommon rhetorical gifts more often than not fall into slothful habits of thought
because their verbal facility carries them through most situations
and wins them much superficial acclaim. Willimon does repeat
stories often—perhaps too often—but although I do not know
him personally, I have the impression from what I have read that
he is always alert for new material, always listening for and
expecting the Spirit to speak through the mundane, always wait-
ing for a fresh insight to spring forth from the scriptural text. His
famous open endings exemplify his faith in the power of the
Word to create something new that is independent of the messenger and out of his control.

We need more *thinkers* in the pulpit. This does not necessarily
mean that we need more superior intellects (although that would
be a good thing too); some of the most effective sermons I have
ever heard were given by men and women of middling intellectual capacity. The *sine qua non* is not the IQ; it is *the habit of reflection*. What we want to see in the pulpit is a person who is
struggling with all his or her might to understand the big, deep
questions raised by the encounter of the Word with the world and
to say something out of that struggle that will feed the sheep. One
suspects that Willimon might have been a glib preacher. By his
renunciation of the easy, thoughtless way, he glorifies God.

I put fearlessness first in this article because it commands
attention. But to repeat, it is *theological* fearlessness. It is the hallmark of the person who knows that "this God will have his sovereign way with us." It arises out of "one's conviction about what
sort of God we have got. Or, more biblically, what sort of God has

got us." Note how Willimon reverses the order of subject and verb; this is a man who is *thinking*. "Faith is known by its subject," he continues. Note that he does not say "its object." God is the initiator, the disrupter, the invader—the acting subject. He is the one who "loves to keep creating, to wrench life out of death, who delights in making a family where once there had been no people (1 Peter 2:10)." This, truly, is the Creator *ex nihilo*.[12]

I have found no evidence that Willimon in his preaching ever loses sight of the Author. It is true that his sermons don't always have God as their subject in any obvious way. But what does become obvious is that this man, this preacher, is saturated with life in God. Without exception he thinks in God-categories. He does not slip in and out of theological thinking. He has drawn absolutely everything into the Christian worldview. In reading many sermons I did not find any exceptions to this—and this is a remarkable thing, because Willimon is a man of the world, not a cloistered scholar or mystic who can simply shut out what is extraneous or distracting. He reads stuff and goes to movies and watches TV and follows the news, so he has a big job to do even as the "mind of Christ" is being formed in him. Preachers who want to emulate Willimon will become voracious readers, watchers, students of the culture—and they will redouble their efforts to make *God* their subject through it all.

An additional sign of Willimon's use of verbs to communicate his theological stance is the way he speaks about faith itself. He has thought about the way that language works. He does not exhort us to have more faith. He does not generalize faith in the manner of those who make "Believe!" a slogan or rhapsodize that "any dream will do." He does not allow us to think of faith as a human work at all. In the sermons I have read, I have not found any direct references to Galatians 3:23-26, but he seems to have internalized it. In this Pauline text, "faith" is either active—the subject of verbs—or the means by which God acts: "Now before *faith came*, we were confined under the law, kept under restraint until *faith should be revealed*. So the law was our custodian until Christ came, that we might be justified *by faith*. But now that *faith has come*, we are no longer under a custodian; for in Christ Jesus

you are all sons of God, *through faith*" (emphasis added). "Faith"
is synonymous with "Christ," as Richard Hays has definitively
shown.[13] In just this way, Willimon frequently, and strikingly,
uses "the gospel" as the subject of a strong verb: "The gospel
demands," "the gospel requires," "the gospel creates." This is rem-
iniscent of a passage from the Epistles where the *evangel* is the
acting subject: "Of this you have heard before in the word of the
truth, the gospel *which has come* to you, as indeed in the whole
world *it is bearing fruit and growing*" (Colossians 1:5-6 RSV,
emphasis added). Willimon makes the gospel itself the acting
agent, for instance when he writes, "The gospel is after bigger
game than merely to 'speak to the contemporary world,' the project that liberalism assumed. The gospel doesn't want to speak to
the modern world. It wants to change it. God's primary way of
change is through words, by bringing a new world to speech."[14]

Willimon has staked his ministry on his conviction that it is
the vocation of the Church to speak in "the grammar of faith"
(appropriating Paul Holmer's phrase). This, too, requires serious
thought and long-term commitment. It is not so easy to develop
fluency in the grammar of faith when everyone around us is
speaking the language of the culture. This problem is particularly
insidious when the cultural language masquerades as "spirituality," a particular concern of Willimon's. The language of biblical
Christianity is "peculiar speech," and if the Church changes the
language in order to accommodate the culture, it is no longer the
gospel. When faith came, the Greek language "was seized" (that
aggressive verb again) and transformed into a new language
describing a new cosmology.[15]

His Sermons Are Radical

Speaking of language, aggression, and cosmology brings us to a
fourth feature of Willimon's work that I will examine in this
essay—his radicality. Speaking from my own perspective as an
Episcopalian, we have not heard a voice like this in my denomination since William Stringfellow's death.[16] It is curious that

Willimon (and Hauerwas) are popular among Episcopalians in a certain sense. Indeed, they acknowledge that Episcopalians have liked their work because of its high ecclesiology. I very often hear them cited by my fellow clergy. Yet these are often rueful citations, as though the persons quoting Willimon and Hauerwas feel themselves to be at a great remove from what they are quoting— admiring it perhaps, finding it attractively pungent certainly, recognizing its value as a corrective no doubt, but nevertheless regarding it from afar as though it were the arctic tundra; it is bracing to think it's out there, but we don't want to live in it. It is a comfort to Episcopalians to think that Church is the primary source of life, but more and more these days, we seem to want it with a reduced amount of Word. Willimon would be one of the first to say that the Eucharist is in itself radical in its overturning of all worldly distinctions, but this must be preached. God is related to the world essentially through speech.[17] "You can only learn to see by learning to say."[18] It isn't enough to get up and repeat, for instance, "We are resident aliens in the world" over and over and expect the congregation to grasp the full implications of such a statement. Much homiletical effort is required to illustrate the way this works day in and day out in the Church. Harder still is showing how the Church sheds the light of its alien existence into the world for the sake of the world.

What do I mean, then, by *radical*?

In a quotation above, Willimon refers to *cosmology* as if in passing, but this conception lies at the heart of his vision. Being the Christian Church means *an exchange of worlds*. Being a disciple of Christ, being a royal priesthood, being the new creation, means signifying "a world where Jesus Christ is Lord [*Kurios Iesous*], where the kingdom of God is beginning to take form, and where their lives are given significance as those who are ambassadors, emissaries, the first wave of God's promised kingdom." It is not possible to overstate the radical nature of this gospel. Willimon uses words like these to describe conversion: *antagonistic, disruptive, disjunctive, discontinuous, dissonant, discordant, disconcerting.* "Radical turning is required, turning that is initiated by *a power or source external to the person being turned.*"[19] This is the theological affirmation that marks the distinction between radical and merely "liberal" interpretations of the New Testament message. The emphasis is on the power of God to overturn one world and speak another into being. It's about spheres of power, not the inner disposition of the heart. By way of contrast, Willimon writes that in liberalism, "Biblical apocalyptic is existentialized, Biblical prophecy is moralized, Biblical narrative is psychologized."[20]

Caricature and ridicule are part of Willimon's arsenal (I envy his ability to get away with this). Instead of capitulating to the current fashions in the Church, he heaps scorn upon them. As a man "commandeered" by Christ he is so thoroughly rooted in the new creation (1 Corinthians 5:17) that he is able to outdo the politically correct evangelists at their own game of civilized disdain, mocking their supposedly liberated but highly acculturated way of dismissing Scripture—"the old, culturally conditioned, sexist, violent, Jewish, premodern Bible and its distance from our fresh, modern, enlightened world . . . standing upon the pinnacle of human development."[21] Since we know Willimon as a man unafraid of talking about sin and human foolishness, we recognize the irony in this reference to "human development."

When Willimon preaches, however, he is not—despite appearances—primarily interested in entertainment, amusement, shock, or even challenge in the usual sense of that word. He is interested in *conversion*. His confidence lies in his certainty that the distant, alien world of the Bible is our true home, and he will not let anything deflect him from announcing that, Sunday after Sunday. That is radicality. If Sunday morning worship is a "clash of narratives," as he puts it, then he will expend himself to the last syllable to deliver the power-filled, Spirit-driven narrative about the exchange of worlds—the world of American individualistic, nationalistic, materialistic, hedonistic consumerism for the encroaching kingdom of God. "Our prophetic testimony is . . . our joyful announcement, in word and deed, that God is bringing all things unto himself in Christ Jesus."[22]

A Methodist colleague once said to me, *sotto voce*, "Methodists are deeply suspicious of radical grace." Willimon's own radicality is on view in his essay about conversion in the Wesleyan tradition, "Suddenly a Light from Heaven." Here is the very best of John and Charles Wesley, not always present in the attenuated versions of Methodism that succeeded them—Willimon's is a sort of Augustinian Wesleyanism free of emphasis on human autonomy. "Moralism," Willimon writes, "is an attempt at self-salvation, to be related to Christ through our earnest efforts rather than through the work of Christ in us. Wesley preached the triumph of grace, the power of grace to make us that which our earnest efforts could not. . . . Sanctification is a work of God in us, a movement from heaven, a light not of our devising, something that is due to God's grace rather than self-derived. . . . [It is] the accomplishment by the gospel of something the Law could never do." There can be no "insufferable, sentimental moralism" here ("making nice people even nicer").[23]

As far as I can tell, Willimon's preaching exemplifies these convictions with remarkable consistency and integrity. As we have noted, his sermons are entirely free of exhortation. Part of his power is his ability to illustrate, to illuminate, to invite—but never to harangue or berate. As requested by the editors, I have chosen two sermons for inclusion in this volume. I am sure that all of the contributors to this book have had the same trouble I have had: We want to include so many! It has been very difficult to select a mere two. However, I have reluctantly made the cut and have come up with two Easter Day sermons. On reflection, I think this is not an accident. In my experience, Easter preaching is the most difficult of all. There simply are not words adequate to the task. Moreover, there are so many popular substitutes for the real thing ready at hand—the preacher can talk about any and everything upbeat, from the spring weather to the plans for rebuilding Ground Zero. He or she can tell stories about people who have surmounted great obstacles, or report on movies like *Field of Dreams* that evoke a sort of afterlife. The possibilities are almost endless. The preacher who wants to affirm the resurrection in all its unique, profoundly affronting uniqueness, however, is reduced to sputtering monosyllables: This thing happened. They went to the tomb. He was not there. God did this. We don't know how he did it. They saw the Lord. He came through the door. He spoke to them. He broke bread. Their eyes were opened. It is a new world now.

I figure I have heard about fifty live sermons by various preachers on Easter Sunday in my adult life (counting Easter Vigil sermons), and I am truly saddened to report that almost all, though not quite all, of them were theological failures. That is to say, the preacher backed off at the crucial point. The key affirmation—"God raised Jesus from the dead and we are witnesses"—was not made. In the end it is tempting to conclude that large numbers of preachers make a conscious effort to *avoid* saying what the Scripture clearly says, substituting various other messages of the sort noted above, messages with more palatable content. You will note, reading Willimon's two Easter sermons, that he does exactly the opposite. He refuses the easier, more reasonable messages in dismissive tones suited to their inadequacy, and then proclaims the unvarnished New Testament gospel of the resurrection of the body in unmistakable terms—take it or leave it, but do not try to blunt its edge. The inverted sentences drive this home: "You can't 'explain' a resurrection. Resurrection explains us."

You will note many other things as you read these Easter sermons.

The news of the resurrection is shocking and confusing, unexpected and even frightening.

It is "according to the Scriptures"; that is to say, it is part of the deliberate purpose of God from the beginning.

The implications of the resurrection have more to do with the future of the cosmos than with resurrection as individual destiny. The question Willimon frames is "What shall be done about the world?" not "How shall individuals be saved from death?"

The passion and resurrection (as single event) is the battlefield where two cosmic forces meet and the Church takes its subsequent stand, so that martial imagery is suited to the situation ("bridgehead, mopping-up actions").

The resurrection was not merely a "spiritual" event, but a resurrection of the body with all that it implies for the significance of earthly existence.

And if there were any doubt left about the point made in the title, "It's About God," let us take note of the numerous affirmations about God—indeed, we could hardly miss them:

- "Easter is about God—a God who raises dead Jesus just to show who's in charge here."

- "God invaded the tomb."

- "God took charge."

- "God inserted a new fact."

In the resurrection of Christ, Willimon is not afraid to announce, "We got our first glimpse of a new world, a world where death doesn't have the last word, a world where injustice is made right, and innocent suffering is vindicated by the intrusion of a powerful God." Notice the climax of the sentence, how it builds up to the confession of a God who intrudes, assaults, invades—with power stronger than that of the Last Enemy, which is Death. No other sorts of words are strong enough. It will be said of Will Willimon as long as the story is told, he did not flinch from his calling. From the pulpit in Duke Chapel as long as we were blessed to have him there, words came forth that were commensurate with their great Subject. Thanks be to God.

A Concluding Word to Developing Preachers

As a coda, I hope I may be allowed this caution to preachers who will be reading this volume with the hope of attaining to Willimon's stature:

My purpose in highlighting four particular qualities of Willimon's preaching is to offer four things that can be learned or acquired. What cannot be learned or reproduced without unfortunate results, in my opinion, are the mannerisms and character-istics that are uniquely his own—the special brand of wit, the abrupt transitions, the famously startling conclusions, and espe-cially the indirection in storytelling (a particularly treacherous technique for the unskilled, and much overused).[24] No one can attain to stature as a preacher without developing his or her own distinctive voice. It is typical of a young preacher to try several different styles before settling into one; that, certainly, is what I did, and the process took a number of years.

It is very tempting to think that one has mastered the craft if one has learned to use the techniques. The opposite is the case. The techniques will become less and less important when habits of thought have been developed. No amount of technique can replace deep reflection on the intersection of Word and world for the sake not of the "saved," but for the sake of the world itself. No trendy new theories can substitute for a lifetime of immersion in Scripture for its own sake, neither for the sake of uncovering its inconsistencies nor apologizing for them, but for the truth and comfort of God's Holy Word. No mastery of rhetorical flourishes will ever compensate for a lack of love between pastor and con-gregation. No fireworks in the pulpit will be able, year after year, to enable the Church to fulfill its arduous, all-consuming counter-cultural vocation of witness and service.

In Willimon's own book addressed to his colleagues, *Pastor*, we find these corroborating words:

> The church [is] a political reality that presents, in its speech, in its life together, in its love for the world, an alternative to the world. The Acts 2, pentecostal test for prophecy is not how outrageous we have managed to be in the pulpit but rather how many people . . . we have produced who are able to say No, people who can speak the truth to power. The real test of preaching is not the praise of the public or even its faithfulness to the original Greek of the Biblical text, but rather the ability of a sermon to evoke a prophetic people.[25]

In Douglas Harink's new book, *Paul Among the Postliberals*—which among other things is a conversation with Stanley Hauerwas—there is a passage about Paul's preaching that well describes the apostolic vocation that Will Willimon has embraced and exemplified. After describing Corinthian society, "thoroughly pagan and idolatrous at every level," Harink continues:

> From this, Paul had to shape a people who would bring glory to the God of Israel. He did so by announcing the good news of how this God had invaded the world of Corinth and its culture through Paul's message about the crucifixion and resurrection of Jesus Christ. A new power was unleashed in the city, a power able to deliver the Corinthians from their enslavements to the many lords, powers, and practices that had laid claim to their lives. God was creating a new people in the midst of Corinthian culture by choosing, calling and setting apart those that believed the message that Paul proclaimed. . . . The body politic of Jesus Christ would thus form a concrete sign of the redemption of Gentile Corinthian culture, in the very heart of cosmopolitan Corinth.[26]

Ad majorem Dei gloriam.

CHAPTER 3

RESIDENT ALIENS: "CHRISTIANITY IS WEIRD, ODD, PECULIAR"

Flag and Cross, Cross and Flag

LUKE 9:51-62

July 1, 2001

In today's Gospel, Jesus is on the way. He is on the way to becoming popular. His movement is really gaining momentum, attracting, in Luke's words, "a great crowd."

And at this point, Jesus is going on ahead, going on to Jerusalem. He is going to his cross. And at this point he begins to teach his disciples where he is going. Do they want to walk with him in that direction?

In verses 57-62, somebody comes up to Jesus and says that he will follow him wherever he goes. Jesus tells him that means to live life without a home.

Another person comes up to Jesus, saying that he will come, but first he must fulfill his family obligations, arranging a funeral for his father. Jesus responds in a sharp, caustic way. Let the dead bury the dead (v. 60).

Following Jesus is not always that easy. Along the way, to the cross where he is headed, Jesus is forever correcting, surprising us—surprising us with how odd, how very different is following than we first imagined. And in this, and on a number of other occasions, Jesus impresses us with how odd, how against the grain his way is when compared to our ways. Here are the nice people, wanting to mix Jesus with their family obligations, their domestic concerns, and here is Jesus, supremely disinterested in their commitments, giving them new commitments, beckoning them to walk a narrow way. His way. The gospel way to life is narrower than we often appreciate.

And one reason we get together on a weekly basis and tell these stories and examine these texts is so that we may more clearly discern his way, more clearly see the difference between his ways and our ways. Isn't family loyalty a good thing? Shouldn't we show respect to our deceased parents? So many times, with Jesus, the problem is in a clash between one good and another. There are many things—like family, like parents, like money—that are all good things. But sometimes, with Jesus, there is a clash with good.

And just as it is difficult to mix oil with water, it can also be difficult to mix Jesus with our values.

A former student of mine at the Divinity School was telling me this summer that she has had a rough year at her first parish. This surprised me because I had heard that she had been well received there when she arrived last year. What was it that was causing the trouble, I asked her.

"Santa Claus," she said.

"Excuse me?" I said.

"My church is in danger of running me off because of Santa Claus. Last December, they told me that they had this tradition in the church, on the second Sunday of December, of having Santa Claus appear at the worship service on the second Sunday in December.

" 'The kids just love it,' they said. 'In fact everybody loves it. It really gets us in the mood with the Christmas spirit,' they told me.

"I did what you told me in class," she said. "I tried to move into this carefully. 'Well, that's an interesting liturgical tradition,' I said. 'But I don't really believe that Santa Claus has any place in a Christian sanctuary. Most of us with young children feel that we've got such a struggle going on with Christmas, the commercialism and all, I don't think we need to do anything else to get our children any more into the Christmas spirit.'

"Santa Claus is fine, but he is not Jesus. It's just so hard for the church to get its message across, with all the Christmas commercial hoopla, I don't think we need to be confusing things, blurring the issues, by having Santa Claus visit us at church."

I can see her point. And I like the way she made it. One of the purposes of church is to get us together to keep clarifying the Christian way. We are bombarded every day by thousands of messages, mostly in the form of advertising, that proclaim a worldview, a way of living, and a system of values that are not Christian. So we get together at church and try as best we can to keep things clear. But it isn't easy.

A couple of years ago I had a painful conversation with a Jewish student who noted, "You've got this Easter thing coming up soon, don't you," trying to make conversation with the preacher.

I responded that indeed the "Easter thing" was coming up in a couple of weeks.

"So tell me," he continued politely, "just what is Easter about, anyway? What do the decorated eggs have to do with it? Did Jesus enjoy decorating eggs? Are eggs some kind of Christian ritual?"

I informed him that the eggs had nothing to do with it.

"So then the bunny—what about the bunny?" he persisted. "Did Jesus like bunnies? Is the bunny some kind of symbol for God or something?"

He put me in an embarrassing position of having to admit that none of that stuff, though dearly beloved and widely celebrated in this culture, had anything to do with the "Easter thing." Of course, he is not of this faith, and so he is not supposed to know about these details, but as a preacher, I had to ask myself about the odd ways we allow extraneous symbols to muddy the waters of our faith, so to speak. It is very hard for us to keep our stuff straight. It is easy to get confused.

A friend of mine says that on Sunday morning, when he stands up to preach, he looks out on groups of people who think that they are Methodist. In reality, a lot of them are Shintos who are worshiping their ancestors buried out in the adjacent church graveyard; some of them are Muslims who believe that every word of scripture was dictated by God Almighty; some are Buddhists who come to church in an effort to get away from the world; others are just plain good pagans who believe that the purpose of religion is to try to get all of the gods to do something nice for us.

But there are those moments when church becomes a place of clarification. We realize that Jesus' way does not mesh easily with every other way. We have to "test the spirits" because not every spirit is the Holy Spirit. We open the Scriptures and we ask the preacher, "Is there any word from the Lord?" Because we have spent all week listening to this cacophony of voices—words that are not God's words.

A couple of summers ago, I was in a little suburban church outside of Berlin. I noticed, as we were going in, that people were pulling up in a large Mercedes unloading a lace-bedecked baby, accompanied by whirring video cameras, so I knew we were going to have a baptism.

Well, we went through the service, and the sermon, and all of the adoring relatives and guests endured this. Then the time came for the baptism. The dour German pastor called everyone to come forward. And a large number of people got up, presenting the baby. Two or three video cameras began to whir.

Then this German pastor said, as best I could translate him, "Stop! We're not in a theater! This is not some sort of theatrical spectacle! This is church. We're getting ready to make a new Christian. We're getting ready to lay the cross over the life of this innocent baby. There is a cost in these matters. This is frightening, holy business. Turn the cameras off. We do not want distractions that might confuse the parents or the church about the solemn, holy thing we are about to do."

As a preacher, I wondered if I would have been so severe, reacted in this way. I doubt that I would have. I am probably a lot nicer than this German pastor. But then I remembered, this is a *German pastor*. His church knows, from sad experience, what it is like to become confused, to have the lines between the church and the world tragically blurred. They came to that point when the church desperately needed to say no! But it had lost the will to resist, had lost even the means to know that there was something in Germany to resist.

Therefore, you must forgive the pastor for his severity. He knew that much was at stake here. The church has got to be careful about distractions.

This spring, I went up to Washington, D.C., to speak at a pastors' conference. After I spoke, Alan Storey, a young pastor from South Africa, led us in worship. Many of you know Bishop Peter Storey, favored preacher from this pulpit, sometime professor at Duke Divinity School. Alan is Peter Storey's son. Alan stood up before us, handed out the bulletins for the service, and walked us through the service. Then he said quietly, at the end of the instructions, "One more thing as we begin our service. Could I just say, as visitor to your country from another place, that I wish you would consider removing the American flag from your sanctuary? I was shocked when I entered this church today and found your country's flag so prominently positioned near the altar. That would not happen in my church. My church law forbids us to have flags and other secular political paraphernalia in our services. I wish you would think about this and how this flag clashes with the symbols of our faith. Of course, I am from South Africa. And we've learned the hard way about the difference between the ways of God and the ways of the world."

We sat there in awkward silence and then went on with the service.

What do you think about that? Does the American flag have a place in our Christian sanctuary?

I fear a confusion of symbols. To Christians, symbols are big. We sit here today surrounded by symbols of our faith. We take symbols seriously because we know the ways that these symbols form us. The symbols don't only *speak* about our deepest commitments, they *form* our deepest commitments. Should a flag be in church?

I expect, when we hear somebody like Alan Storey, we think to ourselves, "Well, he's from South Africa. We're different.

46

We're Americans. We live in a democracy. Our country is good. We're innocent."

I hope none of us would say such sentiments openly, because such sentiments are not true. Our country has blood on its hands. The souls of countless African slaves, of slaughtered Native Americans, and others would rise up and accuse us if we made such arrogant statements about our country. Our nation, like any nation I know of, has blood on its hands; it is far from innocent.

Time and again in Scripture, the great competitor for allegiance to God is allegiance to the nation. Much of the time, when Hebrew prophets condemn false gods and idolatry, they're talking about the false trust we put in kings, in armies, in the mechanism of the state.

It is not enough to say, "We fortunately live in a democracy, where we don't have a king, where the people are king."

Democracy puts us in an even more spiritually demanding situation. Once, we went to war for the king; now we go to war and kill for ourselves. Once, only a king was brutal enough to cut off somebody's head. But just last week, all of us executed a murderer. The government has become our protector from the cradle to the grave, our main source of meaning, that to which we look in life for salvation.

One of the big movies recently was *Traffic*, a revelation of what drugs have done to our culture, in high and low places. Some of the characters in the movie suggest that drugs are a government problem, that the scourge of drug abuse can be solved through wiser government-sponsored treatment programs.

It is typical of us to think that the government is the solution to our every need. For the life of me, I cannot figure out a good government program that could give people ultimate meaning in life, that could keep people from wanting to kill themselves. We ask too much of the government. We sacrifice too much for the nation.

Anybody who would die for a religion is considered a mindless fanatic. And yet, when people sacrifice their lives for the government, we call them heroes. Don't tell me that we shouldn't be careful about bringing the objects of national devotion into our Christian sanctuaries.

In a couple of days we will celebrate the Fourth of July, the birth of our beloved nation, a nation that has been so good to so many of us. On the Fourth of July we celebrate our Declaration of Independence. But "independence" is not a biblical word. Independence is what government promises us, if we will just serve the government. As Christians, our Sunday morning goal is not independence, but rather *dependence* upon the will and the righteousness of God. We Christians are more weird than we often admit.

I hardly ever come to this Sunday in the year, the Sunday before July 4, that I don't remember my visit, about twenty years ago, with my family to a very large church in California. A church with more glass, even, than this one. A church with a much larger TV audience than ours. At any rate, we went through this service. During the service we sang "America the Beautiful," "My Country 'Tis of Thee," and a lot of the songs that one might expect on the Sunday before July 4. There was a children's sermon in which an associate minister came out with a rat puppet that talked to the children about how good it was that we live in America. And when we came to the sermon the preacher at that church was away that Sunday, spreading the gospel in Hawaii, we were told. They had a guest preacher, Charles Colson. A lot of you are old enough to remember Charles Colson of Watergate fame, the trouble that he got into, and the time that he served in prison.

My dear mother, sitting next to me, said, in a voice loud enough to be heard by a number of people near us, "I haven't come here to church to hear some jailbird preach."

I said to her, "But he has had a conversion experience; he has given his life to Christ."

"That's what they all do when they come before the parole board," she said.

At any rate, Charles Colson began to preach. "This is quite a congregation that is arrayed before me," he said. "I wish you could see yourselves and how magnificent you look on this beautiful Southern California day. I wish all of those watching TV could see what a grand and glorious place this church is. Quite a contrast from where I preached yesterday. Yesterday I preached, not in this grand church, but in a little cinderblock building at the Los Angeles Prison Farm. There I preached not to this fine assembly, but to murderers, rapists, thieves. And you do know with which group Jesus was more at home?"

My dear mother leaned over to me and said, "I hope Mr. Colson is having a good time preaching here because he will never be invited back."

The greatest service Christians have to render this nation is to be a critique, a visible reminder that God, not nations, rules the world, that we have a loyalty that qualifies every other loyalty. Jesus Christ is Lord.

Surrounded by a Great Cloud of Witnesses

HEBREWS 11:29–12:2

August 19, 2001

> *Therefore, since we are surrounded by so great a cloud of witnesses, let us also lay aside every weight and the sin that clings so closely, and let us run with perseverance the race that is set before us, looking to Jesus the pioneer. (Hebrews 12:1-2)*

G. K. Chesterton said, "Democracy is the conviction that a man's opinion ought not to be dismissed simply because he is your butler." Tradition is the conviction that a man's opinion ought not to be dismissed simply because he is your father. I want to say a kind word for your parents.

I was meeting one night with a group of students in a dormitory. They had asked me to lead them in a discussion of "Christian worship." At that hour I was greeted by zombielike stares, so I was eager to try to draw students into the subject. Just off the top of my head I asked them, "Those of you who've seen Christians at worship, what would you say is the strangest thing that you've seen? And don't mention the thing about the man in the white dress—something else."

And an undergraduate spoke up and said, "I think the weirdest thing is when, at the beginning, in the opening parade . . . "

"Processional?"

"Yeah, where they bring in that great big book."

"The Bible?"

"Yeah, and they bring it up and put it up on the lectern and you can see the person bringing it in sort of turns toward the clergy and says, 'Here, work from this.' That's weird."

And I thought, thank you for that. That a group of late twentieth-century North American people should gather and, just for an hour on Sunday morning, say, "Let's all believe that these ancient Jews knew more than we do. Let's just try that for an hour, and see where we'll be"—that really is strange. That is not happening everywhere else: that a group of modern people, privileged to stand at the summit of human development—Durham, 2001—that we should gather and submit to these ancient writings. That's very strange.

Let us do something strange: Let's listen to this book, let's read something that was written almost two thousand years ago:

> By faith the people passed through the Red Sea as if it were dry land, but when the Egyptians attempted to do so they were drowned. By faith the walls of Jericho fell after they had been encircled for seven days. By faith Rahab the prostitute did not perish with those who were disobedient, because she had received the spies in peace.

And what more should I say? For time would fail me to tell of Gideon, Barak, Samson, Jephthah, of David and Samuel and the prophets—who through faith conquered kingdoms, administered justice, obtained promises, shut the mouths of lions, quenched raging fire, escaped the edge of the sword, won strength out of weakness, became mighty in war, put foreign armies to flight. Women received their dead by resurrection. Others were tortured, refusing to accept release, in order to obtain a better resurrection. Others suffered mocking and flogging, and even chains and imprisonment. They were stoned to death, they were sawn in two, they were killed by the sword; they went about in skins of sheep and goats, destitute, persecuted, tormented—of whom the world was not worthy. They wandered in deserts and mountains, and in caves and holes in the ground.

> Yet all these, though they were commended for their faith, did not receive what was promised, since God had provided something better so that they would not, apart from us, be made perfect.

> Therefore, since we are surrounded by so great a cloud of witnesses, let us also lay aside every weight and the sin that clings so closely, and let us run with perseverance the race that is set before us, looking to Jesus the pioneer and perfecter of our faith, who for the sake of the joy that was set before him endured the cross, disregarding its shame, and has taken his seat at the right hand of the throne of God.
>
> (Hebrews 11:29–12:2)

I expect that First Church Thessalonica, or First Church Athens, Greece (not Athens, Georgia), or wherever this letter was directed must have felt very much alone. They were a tiny band of Christians, hanging on by their fingernails on the fringes of the great Roman Empire. There had been purges, persecutions, mocking by their pagan neighbors. A tiny, insignificant sect. How on earth could they keep "keeping on"?

The Letter to the Hebrews reminds them. They are not the first to walk this path. Their ancestors in the faith—Gideon, Samson, David—walked before them. They knew torture, prison, death; yet they kept walking in faith, even though none of them received as much for their faith as we have. Remember your grandparents and take heart. They not only walk before you but also with you.

Here is an act of studied remembrance. One of the best ways to keep going forward is occasionally, such as here in the Letter to the Hebrews, to look back.

Neil Postman says that if you teach in a college or university, no matter what you teach, you are a historian. The purpose of higher education, as it's practiced over in the Chemistry Department, as in the History Department, the purpose of all higher education, is history. It's one generation telling another what we found out, what we know.

To be a teacher of any kind is to allow the past to have its way with us. And that's powerful stuff. One reason I think our culture tends to be ahistorical, tends toward a kind of studied amnesia, is that the past is our greatest accuser. Not only our greatest teacher, but also a revolutionary force.

As G. K. Chesterton said, one of the difficulties of modernity is that we keep talking about how free we are. We've freed ourselves from our past. All that does, said Chesterton, is show that we've become slaves to that arrogant oligarchy of those who just happen to be walking about at this moment.

I worry about the Church. Concerning so much of our worship today, so much of current church life, about the worst thing you could say about it is "it's *contemporary*." It is no more than *with* the times. "Presentism."

I was recently at a church of my own denomination, and I came away just frightened, thinking, "Have I seen the future of the Church?" The hymns (songs really), anthems, everything had jettisoned the tradition, our language, our metaphors, and our *stuff*, in favor of something called "contemporary Christian music." And in my humble opinion, what I heard that day, I just don't think will lift the luggage in the future. As people were singing, praising some vague thing called "God," who, as far as I could tell, had never *done* anything or *said* anything in particular, as we were bouncing along praising, I wanted to say, "You know there are people out there today who just found out that their cancer is not responding to treatment, who found out their kids won't do right, that their marriage won't survive, and here we are just bouncing along, grinning, praising God. We've got some good stuff for that kind of thing. Where is it?"

Later, this preacher down in Atlanta, talking about contemporary Christian music, said, "We've had a contemporary Christian service at our church for the past twelve years." I said, "When does the contemporary stop being contemporary? When we go into our second decade of this stuff?" He said, "You mark my word, you've heard it here first, you're going to drive by some Baptist church in Atlanta, and they're going to have, out there on the lawn, an amplifier, a set of drums, a guitar for sale. We will have moved on to some other infatuation."

This summer, a Lutheran told me that in the ELCA, "We are starting to form new churches that have, as part of their mission, the aggressive, loving nurture of traditional Christian worship.

Little mission enclaves out there that do it the old way, because in a weird way, the old way has become the new way."

I just think there is something built into the Christian faith—maybe we get it straight from Israel—but something built in that makes this faith inherently tradition*al* and tradition*ing*.

A sign on the Winchester cathedral in England says, as you enter the church, "You are entering a conversation that began long before you were born, and will continue long after you're dead." To be a Christian partly means that we don't have to reinvent the wheel, morally speaking. We don't have to make up this faith as we go. The saints will teach us, if we will listen. And for modern, North American people, it takes a kind of studied act of humility to think that we actually have something to learn from the saints.

Walter Brueggemann, in his commentary on Proverbs, says, "Israel was the sort of culture that loved its young enough to tell its young what it had heard from God." Israel (the Proverbs embody this), loved its young enough to say, "You don't have to make up the way as you go. You don't have to reinvent the path to God on your own. We'll tell you. We'll show you the way."

So a student asked me one Sunday, "How come we always sing these old hymns in Duke Chapel? I don't know any of these hymns."

And I said, in love, "Well you'll notice that you won't hear any of this kind of music on MTV. This is a different kind of music. You had to get up, get dressed, and come down here at an inconvenient hour of the day to hear music like this. They won't let music like this be played on the TV. It's a very different kind of music. And another reason we do this kind of music is, you check out the Ten Commandments, it says that thing about 'honor your father and mother.' This is our attempt to do that in just this small way. Because to be a Christian is to find yourself moving to a different rhythm, a different beat."

Built right in to Christianity is the courageous determination to be traditionalists, to sit with the saints, and thus participate in one of the most revolutionary activities of the Church.

I was preaching last summer about this time up in Long Island. And I looked out, and there in the congregation, in the front row, was the writer Tom Wolfe. I knew him: Where else would you see someone dressed entirely in a white linen suit? It was Tom Wolfe, which is ironic because I was just reading Wolfe's huge novel, *A Man in Full.*

And after the service I came up and introduced myself, and he said, "You have a beautiful chapel at Duke."

I said, "Really?"

He said "Oh yes, I love it, it's just great. By the way, who are those statues on the door, as you're coming into the chapel?"

I said, "Oh, I wish you hadn't asked that, that's not one of our better things."

He said, "Well who are the people on the right?"

I said, "Oh, well those are famous Southerners, Robert E. Lee, Thomas Jefferson, Sidney Lanier."

He said, "Oh really?"

And I said, "But on the left you've got famous preachers, great preachers of the Church—Wycliffe and Luther and Savonarola. . . ."

He said, "What?!"

I said, "Savonarola."

He said, "I thought that was Saint Francis?"

I said, "No, a lot of people think that—he's a Dominican. He's Savonarola, Dominican friar, Renaissance Florence."

Then Wolfe said, "I'll be damned. Only the Church would pull a stunt like that."

And I said, "Yeah, and then you've got Luther and Wycliffe. . . ." I didn't get his point.

That night, suddenly it hit me—Wolfe's first big novel was *The Bonfire of the Vanities.* The title comes from Savonarola. Remember that he was preaching in Renaissance Florence where the dominant attitude was "onward and upward; we're learning more about humanity; we may be the center of the universe." In the midst of all that comes Savonarola, who would preach these sermons, and say, "All right, everybody out front. We're gonna have a big fire and take those fancy clothes, and take that jewelry, and take all those pagan books; and let's throw them on the bonfire of the vanities. Better for them to burn now than for you to burn in hell." Eventually, for preaching like that, they threw *him* on the bonfire.

But Wolfe's words stuck with me: "Only the Church would pull a stunt like that." Here in the middle of this university campus with these students—onward and upward, and getting my ticket to success and power as this world defines it, and on my way to Wall Street or Rodeo Drive or Pennsylvania Avenue—you come to church, and the first person you meet is Savonarola! He says, "Boys and girls, please, don't go to hell. Take that MBA and put it on the bonfire, please! Please! There's another way; there are alternatives for how you might live your life. Come on! Get free with me!"

"Only the Church would pull a stunt like that!"

In the name of the Father, the Son, and the Holy Spirit, amen.

Resident Aliens: "Christianity Is Weird, Odd, Peculiar, and So Is Duke's Singular Preacher"

Peter J. Gomes

Will Willimon has become the indispensable companion to American preachers who aim to perfect the craft of preaching. On Saturday nights, more preachers go to bed with Willimon than with anybody else, and on Sunday mornings more congregations hear Willimon, although they may not know it, than anybody else. He is a prolific writer, a ubiquitous lecturer, a passionate preacher, and he is able to draw just the right story, anecdote, and illustration from a seemingly inexhaustible supply. Preaching *à la* Willimon is not argument; at its best, it is a kind of seduction. In order to tell *the* story, he tells stories—frequently, but not always, about himself. In doing this, however, and in doing as well as he does and better than most, he never confuses *his* story with *the* story. He makes it all seem so easy, and thus he produces a generation of imitators who have discovered to their cost, and that of their people, that it is not quite so easy as it appears. Preachers as good as Willimon have their admirers, many of whom are privileged to be represented in this book, and yet, in a moment of unlikely clerical full disclosure, we should confess that there is something profoundly annoying about Will Willimon. Why is he so consistently good? How does he make the obvious sound new and original? Why is he, perhaps the busiest preacher in America, nearly always in good form on Sunday? How does he find time to write all of those books, and how is he largely free of those familiar ego issues usually associated with "great" preachers? It is hard to admire, let alone love such perfection; but more than anyone I know, Willimon would recognize the admiration of his friends as perverse. Like the Christian faith he espouses, it is weird, odd, and peculiar.

For all of his twenty years in the Duke University Chapel, Willimon and I have been good friends. I am his senior in this strange business of college preaching, entering now upon my thirty-fourth year in the Memorial Church at Harvard University, but I regard him not only as colleague and friend, but as mentor. For nearly all of his years in the Duke Chapel we have exchanged pulpits once a year. I love to preach from his pulpit in what I wickedly call "St. Nicotine's," and he is regularly welcomed in Harvard Yard by those who seek relief from my unremitting angular Calvinism. I have often joked that our friendship has been based on the fact that in our exchanges we have never had to hear each other preach.

Like most preacherly rhetoric, however, that is not entirely true. When I had the blessing of a sabbatical some years ago at the Duke Divinity School, I sat regularly under his preaching, and there learned that his was the art that concealed art. The highest praise one preacher gives to another is "I could have done that," or the more rueful variation, "Why didn't I think of that?" It is attributed to Oscar Wilde, who cannot possibly be guilty of all the *bon mots* attributed to him, that when he heard a particularly clever remark, he said, "I wish I had said that," to which his interlocutor replied, "You will, Oscar, you will." Whenever we hear and read Willimon, most of us know how Wilde must have felt; and as Wilde is perhaps the most quoted twentieth-century figure, I would suggest that Willimon would qualify for that title among the clergy.

The assignment of this essay has given me the pleasure of reacquainting myself with Willimon, although in the cold medium of print where sermons are not naturally at home. Sermons, as we all know, even those of us who publish too many of them, are meant to be heard, for sound is their natural environment and many do not translate well into print. I know we are meant to regard such giants of the pulpit as Robertson, Brooks, and even Wesley with all due reverence and awe; as well as they read, however, and all do not read well, we know something is missing, lost, untranslatable from ear to eye. Willimon, though, reads almost as well as he sounds, even though there is a distinct advantage to having heard him before one reads him, for it is possible thereby to catch his little southernisms, the oral pleasure he has in telling a tale, the rhetorical and quite subtle theatrical tricks, the pleasurable sight of a little man proclaiming from a pulpit usually too large for him, and the winning, winsome ways of one adept at drawing an audience in like a skilled fly fisherman. These things are lost in their fullness on the page, but we can still discern the pleasure he takes in his work—pleasures taken and given. For both eye and ear Willimon's are comfortable words, not in the sense of consolation and complacency, but in the proper sense of the Prayer Book "comfortable words": words that supply strength and courage, for that is the correct meaning of the word we translate as "comfort" and that is why the words of Jesus are called "comfortable." They make it possible for us to carry on against all odds, and that is what Willimon's preaching does.

It is important to visualize the setting in which he preaches in order to appreciate just how demanding and difficult is his accomplishment. On that setting I can and do speak with some authority, for we both have taken as our vocation preaching in the most self-centered and self-congratulatory community on earth, the modern secular research university. College chapels once represented the highest religious ideals of their foundation, and while Duke is not a church school *per se*, its foundation is rooted in Christian piety of the Protestant and Methodist strain. Its motto, *Eruditio et Religio,* is engraved on every possible flat surface in the gothic fantasyland that is the Duke campus, and the Duke Chapel, larger than life, was, from the day it opened in the early 1930s, one of the architectural marvels of the new South.

On Sunday mornings the Duke Chapel is filled to the doors. The splendid procession of clergy, acolytes, and choir takes nearly ten minutes to get from the narthex to the chancel, and at the end of the service the great carillon, one of the largest in the world, rings out the hymns of a triumphant Christendom that are heard for miles around. All of this is quite overwhelming, but, as Mae West once said of a friend, "There is less here than meets the eye." The Chapel and its panoply, rather than defining the contemporary Christian ambition of the university, is an unavoidable reminder of what is to many now in power a rather distant, parochial, and even embarrassing past. The only object of devotion in the modern research university, its pious origins notwithstanding, is itself. Truth may be invoked, as it often is at Harvard where we claim *Veritas*, in its scientific sense, as our own; but such a truth in the university setting is essentially what we think we are doing in the library and in the laboratory, and certainly not in the chapel. In places like Duke and Harvard, and in hundreds of other formerly Christian schools, chapels and their incumbents are tolerated as relics from another age that might yet prove to be of some use in a new and very different age. The fate of such places is usually to become a concert hall, a museum, or a depot for nonsectarian good works. The preaching of a distinctive Christian gospel, which holds the institutions and its new values to a different and higher standard than its own self-preservation, is hardly encouraged. Like the great orthodox churches of Soviet Russia, too much a fabric of the landscape, chapels in the modern American college seem far removed from their original purpose and something of a rebuke to the present environment. I remember well a Harvard dean pointing to the Memorial Church many years ago, and saying to me with chatty condescension, "If we were starting over again, we wouldn't put it there," meaning in the very center of the Yard.

Well, we are not starting over, and the Duke Chapel continues both to tower over an ever-increasing academic universe and to house a lively preaching ministry, which stands its ground not by sufferance but by right. To the untutored eye it would seem easy to minister in such a place. Willimon has tenure and, more important, does not have a voting congregation with a meddle-some lay leadership; he can, so it seems, do and say as he pleases with all the resources, the bells and whistles, that go with doing so. Preaching in such an environment would seem to be easy, and Willimon could claim success by following the advice not to scare the horses. Such preaching acknowledges the secular sover-eignties—attempts to make good people feel better—and to soften all those angularities that have historically made faith and reason, Athens and Jerusalem, points and places of tension. To win the grudging respect of one's secular superiors in such an environment is a high ambition often accomplished on secular terms, and always with due deference to reason, toleration, and a general culture of nonoffensiveness. Preaching under these cir-cumstances is almost always polite and vividly vague; spirituality is superior to the divisiveness of religion, and all energies should be lent to the breaking down of particularities, peculiarities, and the service of a common social greater good.

By this standard, Willimon is a conspicuous failure. He has no allegiance to a common social greater good. He preaches Jesus Christ, and him crucified. He does not like the anodyne pieties of the book of Proverbs, likening it to a long road trip with one's mother or William Bennett, and prefers the muscular, and not entirely assimilable, convictions of the apostle Paul. His good news is not "I'm okay, you're okay," but rather, "I'm not okay, you're not okay, and that's not good enough." As a preacher, both pastoral and prophetic, Willimon likes to provoke, and what is devastatingly effective about his preacherly provocations is that he "gets" you not by a thunderous confrontation but by a savvy, even sly, good ol' boy insinuation. His sermons are what we call in the trade "sermons that last after lunch."

One key to the success of his preaching at Duke, and well beyond, is the fact that Willimon is smart. He wears his learning lightly, but it is there when he needs it. And often you hear it when you least expect to find it. It is disarming, direct, and equal to that of his most learned colleagues. One would assume intel-lectual competence in a university or college preacher, but often that is neither expected nor desired, because places of learning are inherently suspicious of learned peers: better a poor, dumb, pious chaplain who will stick to his or her pieties and sense of social insecurity, than one who actually understands and excels in his or her citizenship in a community of letters. It was said at Harvard that what most annoyed many of the faculty about Paul Tillich, when he graced the place as a university professor, was his Teutonic assumption of his own intellectual superiority.

Willimon, however, is that most dangerous member of the modern university: a smart believer. Acceptable would be his acceptance of the limitations of the Christian worldview, which would suggest that he was aware of the realities of modernity, but what makes him interesting, and perhaps just a little subversive, is his acceptance of the limitations of the truth claims of a modernity that simply assumes that because its claims are not "religious," they are true, objective, or rational. The Christian faith may not have all the answers, but at the very least it has a long history of asking the right questions and a process of dealing with human failure, frustration, and fear in light of convictions that are not subject to the self-referentialism of the academy and its obsession with brains, success, and power.

Thus, to use one of his most famous aphorisms, Willimon, as university preacher, is himself a resident alien: He is in the university, but not of the university. What he does is remind the academy, in language that it can understand and not ignore, that he represents an alien dimension in its midst, a different set of values. In one of the sermons that appear above he recalls an encounter with the author Tom Wolfe, who was surprised to discover that among the iconography of the great west door of the Duke Chapel, in addition to Wesley and Robert E. Lee, is a statue of Savonarola, the fiery preaching priest of medieval Florence whose bonfire of the vanities gave Wolfe the title for his first great book. Savonarola condemned to the flames the symbols of worldly pagan ambition and success, and for his pains he eventually was consigned to the same flames, a martyr to a too pungent preaching. No one quite knows what possessed the builder of Mr. Duke's chapel to give so prominent a place to such a controversialist as Savonarola, but Willimon noted:

Here in the middle of this university campus with these students—onward and upward, and getting my ticket to success
and power as this world defines it, and on my way to Wall
Street or Rodeo Drive or Pennsylvania Avenue—you come to
church, and the first person you meet is Savonarola! He says,
"Boys and girls, please, don't go to hell. Take that MBA and
put it on the bonfire, please! Please! There's another way;
there are alternatives for how you might live your life. Come
on! Get free with me!"

"Only the church would pull a stunt like that."[1]

Note that this sermon, entitled "Surrounded by a Great Cloud
of Witnesses," has as its text Hebrews 11:29–12:2: "Therefore,
since we are surrounded by so great a cloud of witnesses, let us lay
aside every weight and the sin that clings so closely, and let us run
with perseverance the race that is set before us, looking to Jesus
the pioneer" (Hebrews 12:1-2).

It is instructive to note that this sermon was given early on in
the academic year, for it has the hint of orientation of new people to the ancient traditions of the Christian Church and the traditions of the Duke Chapel. The theme is history, continuity, and
community, and he uses the text to remind his community,
renewed every year by new students, that they are neither alone
nor first to do the peculiar thing of worship.

As is often the case with Willimon, he begins with a college
experience of his own—talking with undergraduates—and he is
quick to note that paradox of twenty-first-century young people
observing others taking seriously the ancient texts of the
Christian community. For some in Willimon's position the situation would be awkward, for how do you make sense of the curious worship forms of Christians to the MTV generation, perhaps
the first truly unchurched generation since pagan times, which
has lost both connection and language? What is to be made of
the requirement, implicit in Christian worship, that we work
with and from old texts written in remote languages in circumstances seemingly far removed from our own? For Willimon, worship is what he calls "studied remembrance," and the essence of

the tradition is to "re-member," or to put back together, that which has been pulled apart. Rather than apologize for the seemingly anti-contemporary mood of worship, particularly as practiced in Duke Chapel, Willimon argues for grasping one's place in the great continuity. The best way to keep going forward, he argues, is to look back occasionally. Thus, in a youth culture saturated with "presentism," which is what most colleges are, Willimon argues for the validity of tradition. "Tradition," he says in a paraphrase of Chesterton adapted for this moment, "is the conviction that a man's opinion ought not to be dismissed simply because he is your father. I want to say a kind word for your parents."

In this sermon, Willimon the contrarian is fully revealed. He takes on the culture of contemporary Christian music and worship in which most of his freshmen have doubtless been raised; and what a thin culture it is, full of happy, clappy praise, club music with a nod to God, and no room for trouble, trial, sorrow, sin, or loss. Such a culture is full of saccharine self-satisfaction, all crown and no cross, which makes Bonhoeffer's "cheap grace" look like the most costly of all things. What does a culture that knows only Easter do with Good Friday?

To the young, such a culture may seem as if it has always been in place, but Willimon's task is to remind them that liturgical innovations, like hemlines, come and go. What remains is not the rhythm of the dance club, but the rhythm of God's faithfulness and human unfaithfulness. The "new" worship that has been around for now nearly twenty years already seems aging, and will not, he notes, "lift the luggage." He tells of a conversation with a Lutheran pastor, who reports on small enclaves of people who see it as their mission to take on the aggressive nurture of traditional Christian worship the old way, "because in a weird way, the old way has become the new way."

The contrarian is not just complaining of the banality of much of what passes for contemporary worship. Were he to do so, he would come off as just another late middle-aged white man who likes the old hymns and doesn't know the new songs: Sinatra versus Elvis all over again. The contrarian is not an antiquarian, however—far from it. He recognizes that the idolization of the moment, "presentism," and the pandering to the arrested development of those who know only the moment, is as dangerous as the nostalgia-mongering of the older generation. Both need to be brought up short to face a future that enables a present endurance. In the book of Hebrews, the Christians are reminded that they can navigate their present troubles, that is, run the race with perseverance, because they are convinced that where they are going is worth running toward, and they are reassured by all the encouraging cheers of those who have run the race before them. What makes the race interesting is that the goal is attainable (we are not alone or on our own in it), and that the encouragement of others, their good example, is good for us. "To be a Christian," he says,

> partly means that we don't have to reinvent the wheel, morally speaking. We don't have to make up this faith as we go. The saints will teach us, if we will listen. And for modern, North American people, it takes a kind of studied act of humility to think that we actually have something to learn from the saints.[2]

One of Willimon's great themes is the prophetic community. In his essay "The Pastor as Prophet: Truth Telling in the Name of Jesus," he reminds us that the Third Person of the Trinity, the Spirit, has given the world a prophetic community and not simply a few outspoken social critics. Pentecost, in the book of Acts, is a communal experience, a gift outpoured on the most unlikely of people who, once nobodies, are now in-spirited to become somebodies. This concept, easily abstracted in the Pentecost discourse, is made real in the sermon addressed to new students in the Duke Chapel. They are made to see themselves as entering upon an adventure long in place before they arrived. In that sermon, Willimon cites a sign outside of Winchester Cathedral: "You are entering a conversation that began long before you were born, and will continue long after you're dead." It reminds me of the motto on the menu of Boston's famous market dining room, Durgan Park: "Founded Before You Were Born."

The young are invited into an ongoing conversation, but they are not meant to be intimidated by the venerable discourse. Willimon wants them to know, as does the book of Hebrews, that this is now their time, their moment to participate. In fact they are encouraged to do so, they are empowered to do so. What strikes him here is that this conversation is transforming; it can change you, and it is to that change that the young are invited.

Now this is easier said than done. First, young college students, especially at places like Duke and Harvard, are easily intimidated by the power and prestige of the institution. They are as grasshoppers in the land of giants. They come to these places to be impressed, and are easily so. Who are they to dare participate as equals in a venerable tradition? They come wanting and willing to be made into whatever Duke and Harvard make best: They are willing to conform, to pay the price, or at least that seems to be the Faustian bargain they have made with the admissions gods. Despite the famous alumni egos, the undergraduates, especially the freshmen, tend to assume that they are the "admissions mistake," and, as each class admitted is presumably smarter than its predecessor, the course of one's career is not good for one's self-esteem.

These are people who at one and the same time think too highly and not highly enough of themselves. If to this you add the sense that college students tend to be inherently conservative and resist embracing changes within themselves or their culture until they can do no other, then you have a paradox ready-made for the contrarian convictions of the gospel as dispensed by the preaching of Will Willimon. Traditionalism is revolutionary for Willimon, as he says in that sermon on witnesses: "Built right in to Christianity is the courageous determination to be traditionalists, to sit with the saints, and thus participate in one of the most revolutionary activities of the church."[3]

He understands, empathetically as well as etymologically, that *tradition* is a verb and not a noun, and thus those who are "traditioned," to use the word as Tertullian would use it, are both fundamentally changed and agents of change. Again, in his essay "The Pastor as Prophet" he makes this same point:

> The goal of the Spirit's descent is the creation of a *polis*, a people who look, speak, and act differently from the world's notion of community. No individual prophets are possible without the existence of a peculiar prophetic community whose life together is vibrant enough to produce a band of prophets who do not mind telling the truth to one another and the world, no matter what.[4]

It was, after all, to ordinary and ignorant persons on the margins of society to whom the gospel first came. In Acts 4:13 the people are impressed with the boldness of Peter and John, "and perceived that they were unlearned and ignorant men, they marveled." This is what Willimon calls "uppity speech," noting that "the prophetic community is composed of young and old, maids and janitors, sons and daughters, those who have not had much opportunity in the world's scheme of things to speak."[5] This is worship, not simply as "feel good," but as empowerment, and Willimon argues that "much Christian worship ought to be predicated on the premise that, if we can get a group of people— elderly people, youth, maids, and janitors—to strut their stuff before the throne of God on Sunday, we will be able to do the same before the city council, or the Pentagon, or the administration on Monday."[6]

Such empowerment effects a change in ordinary people, enabling them, again in the words of Acts 17:6, to "turn the world upside down." Willimon reminds us over and over again that despite the culture of the expert, the elite, and the specialist, when Jesus wanted to change the world, "he summoned a rather ordinary group of inexperienced, not overly-talented folk to be his disciples. This is the typical way Jesus does revolution."[7]

Willimon is often described as a "preacher's preacher." His reputation among the preaching clergy attests to this esteem: preachers love to see and hear someone do well what they try to do. Every cellist enjoys listening to Yo-Yo Ma, every orator admires Lincoln and Churchill. I, however, think of Willimon as a student's preacher, and while he is of inestimable value to the professional clergy, I am convinced that his greatest gift is in transmitting the faith once delivered to the saints to each new querulous college generation in Duke Chapel. Technical and homiletical skills aside, he is able to do well what he does because he is committed to the contrarian convictions of Christian community, to which he invites the young to enter when they have the choice and temptation not to.

I suspect they find his contrariness provoking. He can make people angry. It takes a certain amount of courage to preach that *independence* is not a biblical word, as he did in the sermon that appears above, "Flag and Cross, Cross and Flag": "Independence is what government promises us, if we will just serve the government. As Christians, our Sunday morning goal is not independence, but rather *dependence* upon the will and the righteousness of God. We Christians are more weird than we often admit."[8]

In a culture that finds it virtually impossible to separate the kingdom of God from the best interests of the United States, to argue that we are aliens, strangers, and sojourners in our own native land, having our citizenship in heaven to which we owe our allegiance, and to which as followers of Jesus we must conform, is nothing short of weird, odd, peculiar, and downright dangerous. "The greatest service Christians have to render this nation is to be a critique, a visible reminder that God, not nations, rules the world, that we have a loyalty that qualifies every other loyalty. Jesus is Lord." That is how he ends that Fourth of July sermon. Savonarola could be no more provocative in Florence than Willimon in full cry at the center of the Research Triangle. Those who ignore him, or merely tolerate him as one more harmless Methodist, do so at their peril.

Willimon has convictions about the Christian faith and often quotes his profane and brilliant collaborator, Stanley Hauerwas, to the effect that the Church does not *have* a social ethic, the Church *is* a social ethic. This means that a Christian is not just like everybody else; a Christian is a member of the prophetic community that believes that because Jesus is Lord, the believer and the world must be held to a higher, different standard. This is the nonconformity of Paul in Romans 12, where he invites, beseeches people not to be conformed to this world, but to be transformed by the renewing of their minds. It is the engagement of the mind in renewing transformation that I suspect appeals to the university preaching of Will Willimon, for the mind, both for him and for Paul, is nothing of which to be ashamed. As George Buttrick once famously said, "The door of the college chapel should not be so low that one is compelled to leave one's head outside." The cavernous nave of the Duke Chapel, built perhaps to the glory of the Dukes and in memory of God, is still large enough for the biggest heads to be transformed by the renewing of their minds. Preaching, for Willimon and those who hear him, is indeed a "head-trip."

Ultimately, however, it is the community of Christ, in mind and in heart, that his preaching nourishes: His preaching is prophetic, pastoral, and patient. Patient, I say, for Willimon understands that the work of regeneration is daily work and not the work of a twinkling of an eye: "Daily we turn. Daily we are to take up the cross and follow. Daily we keep being incorporated into the Body of Christ that makes us more than we could have been if we had been left to our devices."[9] The Methodists call this sanctification, an old-fashioned term from which Willimon does not shy. He says of it: "Sanctification is a work of God in us, a movement from heaven, a light not of our devising, something that is due to God's grace rather than self-derived."[10]

Willimon is often hard on his Methodist tradition, arguing that cultural Methodism's chief contribution to theology is the notion that God is nice, but when all is said and done, Willimon is a Wesleyan of the first and best order. He believes that preaching is a part of God's desire for us to desire God. Thus, he writes in the close of his essay on the Methodist doctrine of sanctification:

> When Methodism fails to stress Wesley's conviction of the powerful, even prescient, grace of God as the source of all possibility of new life, Methodism degenerates into insufferable,

sentimental moralism in which the Christian life is depicted as simply another helpful means of making nice people even nicer. Discipleship is not a sanctimonious twelve-step program. A holy person is a testimonial not to the innate possibility within people, but rather to the insistent, transforming love of God in Jesus Christ despite our sin.[11]

Now, all of that may be weird, odd, and peculiar, especially from one paid to preach to the cultured despisers of religion in the modern research university, Methodist roots notwithstanding. It is, however, just the kind of preaching that captures the imagination and attention of those who think they have heard it all before, who have "been there and done that." Hearing it, these young people, perhaps not quite ready to turn the world upside down, might be enticed to begin the hard work of turning themselves around. No preacher can ask for more than that.

CHAPTER 4

DISCIPLESHIP: "I CAN'T BELIEVE YOU PEOPLE ACTUALLY WANT TO BE CHRISTIANS"

Christianity: Following Jesus

MARK 10:35-45

October 22, 2000

Last year, Holy Week, Reynolds Price gave a reading of his translation of the Gospel of Mark, the Gospel we've been reading this year. It was a memorable evening. It took Reynolds about an hour and a half to do it. When he finished, a graduate student and I walked out together. He asked me, "Did they ever get the point?"

"Who?" I asked.

"His students. Jesus' disciples, did they ever get the point? Did they ever get it right?"

"No," I replied, "it's the Gospel of Mark. They never get it right. And I guess that you'd have to be a contemporary follower of Jesus to know that we just love the Gospel of Mark for that reason alone."

And today, we're in Mark, again. And again, no one seems to get the point. James and John ask Jesus to let them sit with him in glory, asking the same Jesus who told them that he is headed for a humiliating cross. They said, "But Jesus said to them . . . " (10:38).

There's a lot of that in Mark. "But Jesus said to them. . . ." He's con-stantly correcting. They just never seem to get the point.

I have poked fun at sermons that seem to have as their theme: "Nine reasons you are not really a Christian even though you may have thought you were when you came to church."

I want to say something this morning about following Jesus. I can't recall any moment when Jesus said to his disciples, "Believe the following five things about me."

No. What Jesus said was, "*Follow me.*"

It is more important to be a disciple, a follower of Jesus, even than to be a Christian. Christianity is not a set of beliefs, first principles, propositions. It is a matter of discipleship, following. Faith in Jesus is not beliefs about Jesus. It's a willingness to follow Jesus. The faith is in the following.

We make a mistake to make this into some sort of mystery. Jesus did not demand that we swallow a dozen philosophical absurdities before breakfast in order to be with him. He asked us to follow. Faith in Jesus is not first of all a matter of having felt something, or having had an experience; it is a simple willingness to stumble along behind Jesus, a willingness to be with him, though behind him. The faith is in the following.

There is therefore no need for any of you to be befuddled by the simple question, "Are you a Christian?" It's a freebie. Easy.

The answer is simply to say, "Yes, I'm trying to follow Jesus. I'm his apprentice, his disciple." The faith is in the following.

If you ask someone, "Are you a carpenter?" there is no need for hesitation. You may not be the world's best carpenter or the most experienced worker in the world. You may have been a carpenter for only two weeks or for as much as twenty years, but the evi-dence that you are or are not a carpenter is simple and self-evident: Are you, or are you not, disciplining your life (discipline = disciple) to the skills, insights, and practices of carpentry? Case closed.

If you asked, "Are you a really good carpenter?" then there might be more hesitation. You are growing as a carpenter, but you are not perfect. But the hesitation does not indicate that you are not a real carpenter. Rather, your hesitation shows that you are a true disciple of carpentry in that you respect how demanding the skill can be. You are still growing, still on the way, still being perfected in the tools of the trade. A beginning carpenter is still a carpenter.

How often in all the Gospels, especially in Mark's Gospel, you hear Jesus criticizing and chastising his disciples! He is often exasperated that they don't get the point, that they fail to follow or they misunderstand. Jesus' criticism of them does not mean that they are not real disciples. It means that they are disciples on a journey. They are on the way. If they had not committed themselves to follow Jesus, if they were not linked to him and his way, there would be no need for correction. Faith does not mean they have arrived, it means that they are on the way.

A person who wants to be a carpenter must apprentice to a master carpenter, minding the moves, inculcating the practices, being attentive to the principles of the trade, willing to be criticized by the master until the apprentice becomes what the master is and does what the master does. That's surely what Jesus means when he says simply, "Follow me."

I recall participating in a discussion where people were asked, "When did you become a Christian?"

People took turns sharing some rather dramatic accounts of how they had been converted into the Christian faith. Some recalled soul-stirring moments when their lives were dramatically disrupted by an infusion of the grace of God and they decided to follow.

But one man, with more than a bit of hesitation in his voice, said, "I can't remember when I wasn't a Christian. I was put here as a child, from the first."

My point is that the imitation of our apprenticeship, the way we got on the journey with Jesus, is not the crucial matter. The crucial matter is that we are on the way.

To be on the way means to be, as a disciple, imitating the moves of the master. Some years ago, I read a book of meditations for Christian college students. The book began, "As a Christian, who is also a student, your task is to be an excellent student. Your discipleship means that you should study conscientiously and thoroughly."

Wherever you are, whatever you do, you are a disciple of Jesus. That's one reason I can't stand that phrase "full-time Christian service" as a way of distinguishing between clergy and laity. Following Jesus is not a matter of learning to do a few religious things on top of the things we do, but rather a matter of doing all that we do, not for ourselves, but for Jesus.

That's surely why Jesus' parables are stories about real life and his teaching is about matters like anger, forgiveness, ordinary injustice, disappointment—the stuff of real life—because he surely meant us to follow him now, in this life, not some other.

I know a barber who, after a lazy day of cutting people's hair for money, goes out to a hospital for the mentally ill and cuts hair for free. A friend of his is an accountant who, after a long day of serving people's financial interests, goes out at night to cruise local bars, pick up women for one-night stands, and enjoy himself as much as possible.

Both men, the barber and the accountant, are apprentices, people attached to some vision of what life is about, why we were put here. One is attached to Jesus. The other is attached to hedonism. So the most interesting question to ask them is not the abstract, "What do you believe in?" but the more concrete, "Whom are you following?" Faith is in the attachment, the following.

The world is right in judging Jesus on the basis of the sort of lives he produces. The only "proof" we have of the gospel, the acid test for the validity of the gospel, is whether or not it is capable of producing lives that are a credit to the Master to whom we are apprenticed.

I've got a friend who is a lawyer by trade, but if you want to name him at his deepest level, for who he really is, he would want you to say that he's a banjo player. He fell in love with the banjo years ago. Then one summer he acted upon his affection, took a month off, signed on with a master banjo player in the mountains of North Carolina. For a month, he lived the banjo. Returning home, he set aside time every day to practice the banjo. He has a set of exercises by which he builds up his hands. He listens to recordings of famous banjo pickers of the past. He spends every other weekend going to folk music conventions to perfect his art. Of course, he's not a perfect banjo player. He still misses a note here and there. He's never been asked to play the banjo professionally, or for money, or full-time.

But he is as much a banjo player as one could ever be. His life has been transformed, changed forever through his art. His daily routine is disciplined in accordance with the demands of the banjo and its music. He is a credit to what the banjo can do for a person who dares to submit to its demands. He hasn't yet fully mastered the banjo, but the banjo has gone a long way to nearly mastering him.

I want you to take this as a parable about following Jesus, about being a Christian, about being a disciple.

Spin City Jesus

LUKE 14:25-33

September 9, 2001

Now large crowds were traveling with him; and he turned and said to them . . . (Luke 14:25)

What does it take to attract people to church these days? About ten million dollars. At least that is what my denomination, the United Methodist, plans to spend on a nationwide advertising campaign to attract new members. "Igniting Ministry," they call this media blitz, translated "Oh my, we're dying. Let's buy some TV time and beg for new members."

Having been at the national gatherings of United Methodists last year, I got to see—repeatedly, redundantly—all of the TV ads that the church is proposing to expose to the American public. One has rain dribbling down a gray-looking window, voiced over with, "Today is my birthday. I'm forty, and I don't know where I'm going."

I didn't get that one. I thought it was an ad for a Cadillac with one of those computerized navigational systems. No, it ended with, "You are welcome at your local United Methodist Church." Then there was one with a woman who said she was tired of people telling her what to do, which I thought was an ad for Prozac. No, it ended with, "The United Methodist Church—open doors, open minds, open . . . " something else—I forgot.

One clergy cynic, after the session, summed up these church ads with, "Self-centered, whining yuppies of the world, have we got a church for you!" Another noted that the dozen ads, attempting to entice people to church, never once mentioned Jesus!

Well, there's a reason for that. What sort of TV ad would you devise to encapsulate today's encounter with Jesus?

> Now large crowds were traveling with him; and he turned and said to them, "Whoever comes to me and does not hate father and mother, wife and children, brothers and sisters, yes, and even life itself, cannot be my disciple. Whoever does not carry the cross and follow me cannot be my disciple. For which of you, intending to build a tower, does not first sit down and estimate the cost, to see whether he has enough to complete it? Otherwise, when he has laid a foundation and is not able to finish, all who see it will begin to ridicule him, saying, 'This fellow began to build and was not able to finish.' Or what king, going out to wage war against another king, will not sit down first and consider whether he is able with ten thousand to oppose the one who comes against him with twenty thousand? If he cannot, then, while the other is still far away, he sends a delegation and asks for the terms of peace. So therefore, none of you can become my disciple if you do not give up all your possessions." (Luke 14:25-33)

I love the way our text begins: "Now large crowds were traveling with him." Jesus, after a shaky beginning at his hometown synagogue in Nazareth (Luke 4), is at last catching on. Crowds, large crowds, are now trooping along behind him. What better validation for Jesus' ministry than this? Crowds.

You, crowded in here on a Sunday, are certainly my best line of defense against any who would dare criticize my work. Somebody doesn't like my sermon, somebody is put off by my ministry, I say, "Did you see how many people were here last Sunday? I must be doing something right? Right?"

At a gathering of clergy one of the speakers was criticizing the work of a certain preacher in Texas with a large TV following. Somebody rose to the preacher's defense. "Are you aware that over two million people tune in to him every Sunday?" Well, his congregation was certainly bigger than ours. End of criticism.

Jesus has got crowds, and right then, in the face of such success and popularity, right there when at last the public opinion polls were running with him, right then, "he turned and said to them. . . . " He turned and said. You can just see Jesus determinedly brisking along as he loved to do, and one of his disciples says, "Master, take a look at that crowd! We must be doing something right!"

And Jesus turns, looks back. "Crowds? I think I can handle a crowd. Don't enlarge the parking lot yet. Crowds?"

And he says to them, "Are you looking for deeper meaning in life? Would you like to be able to approach your work with more enthusiasm? Is this your fortieth birthday? Does your marriage need a boost?"

No. This is Jesus. He says, "Whoever comes to me and does not hate father and mother, wife and children, brothers and sisters, yes, and even life itself, cannot be my disciple."

The crowd gets real quiet. "Did he say, 'hate'? I thought Jesus was into love," asks somebody toward the rear of the congregation. One of his disciples, a theologian, attempted to explain, "He doesn't literally mean to 'hate' your mom and dad. He means rather, 'Keep your old lady in proper perspective.' That's what he means."

Jesus is on a roll and, despite the attempts of his publicists to put a good spin on this PR disaster, nobody can stop him. "Another thing, if you won't carry a cross, you can't walk with me. Anybody who begins to build a tower without counting the cost runs the risk of looking stupid when he runs out of brick and can't finish the tower. Any king who goes to war without first considering whether or not he has the troops to win the war may look dumb as he begs for peace. Count the cost. One more thing, before this sermon's done: You can't be my disciple if you don't give up everything you own."

Wow! The next verse after this sermon, though not included in all of your translations of the Bible, is this: *The great crowds got a great deal smaller after this sermon!*

As far as I can tell, public discourse in our society is now owned entirely by advertising. We are a culture of omnivorous desire.

Our conversation tends to be limited, even at college, to "Here are my needs, appetites, yearnings, and desires; now, how can I fulfill them?" Everything, everyone exists only to satisfy my relentless need, with no critique of which needs are really worth having.

I saw a billboard this summer, put up by some college, saying, "We've got what you want. Now come get it!"

The cynic in me thought, I work with college students, and I know some of the things they want, many of which are immoral, if not illegal. A college is giving them that? We have no higher purpose for any of our institutions—colleges, hospitals, churches—than to satisfy our unformed desires. So we build a car called "Infinity" and tell you that, if you'll just buy one of these babies, you'll have a reason to get out of bed in the morning.

Jesus clearly, at least in this text, has no interest in "meeting our needs." Rather, he appears intent upon giving us needs we would not have had, had we not met him. He speaks of severance from some of our most cherished values—after all, who could be against motherhood, family, and self-fulfillment?

Jesus, that's who.

The *Duke Chronicle* censors any news that has anything to do with religion, so the Chapel is forced to pay thousands of dollars each year to buy advertising space in the *Chronicle* to tell what's happening in religious life on campus. I find this annoying. Even the *Durham Herald* will occasionally report religion.

Yet when we finally scrape together the funds to buy an ad in the *Chronicle*, what are we to say?

Are you happy, content, well situated? Come to the Chapel this Sunday and Jesus will relieve you of all that!

Hate your mother? Trying to get rid of your father? Jesus wants you for a disciple!

What are you doing this Sunday at eleven? Would you like to be crucified?

Can you now understand why our advertising budget at the Chapel is less than that of the Medical Center?

I tell you, when you think about some of the stuff Jesus said (consider his sermons, his demands), it's no wonder to me that

Jesus has trouble attracting a crowd. Even though some of us preachers degenerate to the level of Jesus' "spin doctors," it's a wonder to me that any of you are here on a Sunday.

Unless—unless what Jesus says just happens to be true because he is the way, the truth, and the life. I didn't say that he was the way that nine out of ten thinking Americans want to walk. I didn't say that he was the truth that we think we want, or his disciple-ship was the life we seek. We can't have a good Jesus advertising campaign because his way is decidedly against the crowd. The only reason we're here is not out of our seeking, our wanting. We're here because, in some surprising way, *he* has sought us, wanted us, called us to walk a way not of our own devising. And against all reason or reservation to the contrary, we believe, despite its patent absurdity, his is the way, though narrow, that leads to life eternal.

Forgive me, forgive the Church, for sometimes implying that Jesus will make life easier for you, will fix everything that's wrong with you, will put a little lilt in your voice, a little sunshine in your life. Chances are, he won't. He can do even better than that. He can make you a disciple. Forgive the Church for sometimes being guilty of false advertising.

I was out at a friend's church on the West Coast. We were having a discussion with a group of laity about some of these matters related to Jesus. We were talking about Jesus and his teaching. During the discussion, this angry, loud woman stood up (I told you this was the West Coast), and said to the pastor and everybody else, "I will never again do what some man tells me to do— *unless he's the Son of God!*"

Willimon on Discipleship: "I Can't Believe You People Actually Want to Be Christians"

Thomas G. Long

In the days of my youth, I had a neighbor friend who became concerned about the state of my soul. First, there was this problem with my baptism. Done Presbyterian-style, my baptism was not only water-impoverished, it was also performed on me when I was in a state of infantile semiconsciousness. From my friend's hard-shell Baptist perspective, this was at best biblically improper and at worst eternally dangerous. It was believer's immersion, he was persuaded, or it was nothing. Then there was the issue of my language. My seventh-grade, swaggering street talk, with an occasional daring "hell" or "damn" blurted out in the heat of shirts-and-skins pickup football games, sounded to my friend less like King James and more like Jesse James. One glance at me, and the needle of my friend's fundamentalist faith-o-meter pointed to "sub-Christian."

Since I was in spiritual peril, my friend would beg me to go with him on Friday nights to Youth for Christ rallies, and, because I wanted to stay friends, I would go. In those days, Youth for Christ was a combination of a Cane Ridge revival and American Bandstand. Upbeat music, jokes, games, and skits served as a gentle and seductive prelude to some the most ferocious, sweaty, come-to-Jesus preaching I have ever heard, much of it on the theme, "For all have sinned and come short of the glory of God, especially you."

Most of this was fortunately utterly forgettable, but some things linger. Decades later, I still recall with astonishment the preacher who spent thirty minutes working the logic that Jesus, since he was God's perfect Son, had the most impressive physique of any person who ever lived. I weighed about ninety measly pounds at the time and had the legs and arms of a praying mantis, so this picture of a ripped Jesus was not comforting.

Also riveted in my memory is the sermon that proclaimed, in what I soon discovered was a Youth for Christ mantra, that it was not enough just to "be saved." No, the real measure of one's Christianity, the preacher claimed, was to become a "spiritual grandparent" by passing the faith along through witnessing. (The fact that I was there to hear this sermon was evidence that my friend had taken this message to heart.) "When you accept Christ," the evangelist shouted, "you're born again. When you witness to somebody else and that person is born again, you become a spiritual parent. When their witness saves still others, you become a *grandparent in Christ!*" This was confusing. We had just seen a skit warning us that Jesus didn't approve of petting, and now they wanted us to be grandparents.

As misguided as much of this was, it was also touching and, in its own way, lasting and formative. Forget for a moment the interpersonal naïveté forget the psychological myopia, forget the pinched theological worldview. It was touching that my friend worried about my eternal destiny and not just my ability to spiral a pass. It was touching that these preachers would spend their Friday nights trying to get the gospel across to hormone-hyped teenagers, touching that they wanted us to have the kind of faith that gave us enough courage to stand up against the culture and to speak the name of Jesus, touching that they wanted us to have a faithful influence on the generations to follow. Although I have no desire to backtrack through that phase of my religious development, I will say of those Friday night Youth for Christ rallies: They were about something that mattered—they were about life and death. And I will say of my friend: He cared for me at a depth rarely found elsewhere in our society.

Many years later, I gained a new and cherished friend, Will Willimon. There is very little to compare between my Youth for Christ friend and Will. Will is an articulate, sophisticated, theologically astute minister with a glistening publishing record and long years of distinguished service in pulpit and academy. But my friend Will, too, is concerned about my soul—and about your soul, too. Willimon has never in his life tantalized teenagers with a sweaty Friday night barn burner about a Jesus with perfect abs, but as the chaplain at Duke University, he does expend enormous energy on the formidable task of trying to get the gospel across to adolescents. Moreover, as a seminary professor who has taught a number of students who have been drawn to ministry because of Willimon's influence on them, I can testify that Will has filled the role of spiritual "parent" and "grandparent."

Like my neighbor friend, Willimon is not afraid, in the name of his faith and in order to encourage discipleship, to run counter to the prevailing culture. In print, in the pulpit, and from the podium, Willimon has said some outrageously provocative things. Usually his winsome way and his quick wit earn him some slack from his interlocutors, but occasionally he leaves the hall in an uproar. Most of all, Will Willimon, like my childhood friend, knows that the gospel is about life and death, and not just for the "unchurched" but for the Church as well. Willimon is not reluctant, as he would say, to be intrusive—to stand up in public and to insist that a life worth having, a life worth living, must wrestle with the call of Jesus, which is itself intrusive. "I contend," he once wrote,

> that through evangelism, through repeated confrontation with the intrusive grace of God, the church can be born again. By letting God use us in God's never-ending pursuit of the unbaptized, the baptized can rediscover what it means for us to be the church, that unlikely gathering of those who are called to be sign, signal, and witness to the graciousness of God in a world dying for lack of salvation.[1]

In Willimon's preaching, this urgency of the gospel is expressed in the constant emphasis on the theme of discipleship. The tall and fruitful tree of Willimon's theology has taproots in southern evangelicalism, and Willimon wants people not merely to become Christians but to become disciples, followers of Jesus. The Jesus he urges us to follow is not a guru or a coach or a therapist, but one who walks a hard and dangerous path toward life with God. Jesus' way does not lead to a recliner but to a cross. So, with one hand Willimon beckons his hearers to become followers and students of Jesus, while with the other he cautions them about following too quickly, too nonchalantly, mindless of the cost. "Follow Jesus," he seems to say, "but keep in mind that Jesus has nowhere to lay his head. Go to school with Jesus, but the student parking lot doesn't have room for your Lexus."

Get Behind Me, Yuppies

Any attempt to explore the theme of discipleship in Willimon's sermons must face the fact that his preaching ranges widely in terms of content and style, and his sermons cannot be easily categorized. Like most able weekly preachers, Willimon is not standing in his pulpit in splendid isolation spinning out a series of completely consistent messages with carefully crafted, logically tight systematic theology. He is standing knee-deep in the raging river of current events, trying to give guidance and insight from the Scripture to an ever-changing gaggle of hearers who, in one moment, constitute a Christian congregation on pilgrimage and, at the next moment, resemble a parade of tourists willing to tolerate a sermon for the pleasures of sightseeing in Duke Chapel. One week he opens the door with a smile and preaches a gentle and funny sermon on hospitality, and the next week he's standing at the entrance with a flaming sword and a jeremiad on his lips.

However, despite this flux in sermon topic and approach, one can nevertheless hear over and again the drumbeat of certain themes in Willimon's preaching. One of these is the need for people to leave behind their currently cherished attitudes, biases, prejudices, and lifestyles and to turn in repentance to the way of Jesus. He says,

> When you join Rotary they give you a handshake and a lapel pin. When you join the church we throw you in the water and half drown you. Ponder that. Whatever signing on with Jesus means, it means that we will not do just as we are, that change is demanded daily, sometimes painful turning and detoxification that does not come naturally.[2]

Willimon is a linguistic artist and an engaging pulpit presence, but under the rhetorical finesse stands the classic Christian call, salted with a pinch of Methodist-style holiness, to repent, to turn around, and to follow Jesus in the paths of obedience. His theme scripture verse might well be, "For all who exalt themselves will be humbled, but all who humble themselves will be exalted" (Luke 18:14).

This may sound like typical pulpit fare, albeit skillfully executed, but things get more complicated and interesting when we recognize that Willimon sees himself as preaching not to humanity in general but to well-educated, affluent, post-Enlightenment, late-modern, technologically fueled, media-saturated consumers—or as he might put it, twenty-first-century yuppie pagans. Duke Chapel is not Calcutta, and in Willimon's view, his hearers are suffering not just from the sort of human cussedness that has stubbornly prevailed throughout history, but from a peculiarly American upper-middle-class disease. In contemporary American culture, something of a perfect storm of self-absorption has formed, born of the low-pressure front of basic selfishness, merged with a wave of narcissistic preoccupation with the individual as the arbiter of all moral judgments and the tidal surge of lust for material possessions. "As far as I can tell," he says in one sermon, public discourse in our society is now owned entirely by advertising. We are a culture of omnivorous desire. Our conversation tends to be limited, even at college, to "Here are my needs, appetites, yearnings, desires, now how can I fulfill them?" Everything, everyone, exists only to satisfy my relentless need, with no critique of which needs are really worth having.[3]

Willimon believes that, in the face of this restless craving for self-fulfillment, he is called to preach the hard gospel of a "prickly" Jesus who beckons us to pick up a cross. Theologian Karl Barth claims, in effect, that the Word of God says a loud no before it says a gentle yes, and, indeed, when Willimon has a discipleship sermon in his bones, his Jesus initially comes across less as a gentle shepherd and more as a demanding taskmaster. "Jesus clearly . . . has no interest in 'meeting our needs,'" he states. "Rather, he appears intent upon giving us needs we would not have had, had we not met him. He speaks of severance from some of our most cherished values—after all, who could be against motherhood, family, and self-fulfillment?" Jesus, that's who. "Forgive me, forgive the church, for sometimes implying that Jesus will make life easier for you, will fix everything that's wrong with you, will put a little lilt in your voice, a little sunshine in your life. Chances are, he won't. He can do even better than that. He can make you a disciple."[4]

Willimon is aware that one of the difficulties of preaching on discipleship in his environment is that he is not exactly preaching, as Schleiermacher observed, to the "cultured despisers of religion," but, more precisely, to the cultured admirers of tasteful religion. The reason Willimon so often uses the sharp word and the barbed saying is not just a matter of temperament but of strategy, since he sees his hearers clad in thick armor. With their residual hometown piety, their vague hunger to be "spiritual but not religious," and their desire for an aesthetically pleasing worship experience driving them to church, his hearers have life in perfect balance—a lot of money, culture, and privilege and a little bit of self-reflective spirituality. "Jesus loves me, this I know, for the Duke admissions committee tells me so." Willimon once described the task of Sunday morning preaching as "a clash of narratives." In other words, Willimon lives in a two-story world: the culture has its story, and we have the gospel story, and "the one who gets to tell the story is the one who determines the politics."[5]

At first glance, Willimon, with his wit and well-spoken manner, looks like the perfect chaplain to the cultural *zeitgeist*. But he is on a mission to afflict the comfortable, and he has, hidden in the folds of his pulpit robe, a sermon on discipleship. His hearers come in wearing the look of success; he wants them to leave carrying a cross.

A Vast Conspiracy

As Willimon sees it, then, the main impediment to discipleship is that many of his hearers have much and, nurtured by the prevailing philosophy of self-gratification, want even more. One would expect, of course, this cultural voraciousness to be fed by the marketplace, but the very institutions that ought to teach deeper values and richer practices, those social institutions that ought to support (or at least tolerate) religious impulses, have themselves become infected with the same deceptive, destructive, and self-congratulatory virus. As a preacher who calls for discipleship in the name of Jesus, Willimon struggles not only against flesh and blood but also against powers and principalities, and he must contend with a vast conspiracy of forces and agencies all arranged along the axis of consumerist desire and individualistic arrogance.

Thus, a key aspect of Willimon's preaching on discipleship involves his ambivalent view of institutions. Willimon is persuaded that society's most sacred institutions (such as the family, the school, and the church), charged with the responsibility to nourish people, to sustain society, and to develop vocation, have themselves become infected with the same self-indulgence characteristic of the people who inhabit them. Thus Willimon is a university dean critical of the university, a deeply committed family man critical of the American family, and a devoted churchman critical of the Church.

It may seem odd that his keenest disappointment is saved for the contemporary university and The United Methodist Church. After all, he is a university chaplain and a United Methodist minister, but perhaps this is the key to understanding the sharpness of his criticism. These are the sacred institutions of our culture, and if they have failed us, we have been failed indeed.

When Willimon spotted a billboard, erected by some college, promising, "We've got what you want. Now come get it!" it provoked Willimon to say,

> The cynic in me thought, I work with college students, and I know some of the things they want, many of which are immoral, if not illegal. A college is giving them that? We have no higher purpose for any of our institutions—colleges, hospitals, churches—than to satisfy our unformed desires. So we build a car called "Infinity" and tell you that, if you'll just buy one of these babies, you'll have a reason to get out of bed in the morning.[6]

When Willimon's beloved United Methodist Church launched a $10 million nationwide Madison Avenue-style media campaign designed to attract a generation alienated from the Church, Willimon was outraged by what he saw as a pandering, watered-down message tailored to the egocentricity of the audience. He preached:

> Having been at the national gatherings of United Methodists last year, I got to see, repeatedly, redundantly, all of the TV ads that the church is proposing to expose to the American public. One has rain dribbling down on a gray-looking window, voiced over with, "Today is my birthday. I'm forty, and I don't know where I'm going."

I didn't get that one. I thought it was an ad for a Cadillac with one of those computerized navigational systems. No, it ended with, "You are welcome at your local United Methodist Church." Then there was one with a woman who said she was tired of being told what to do by people, which I thought was an ad for Prozac. No, it ended with, "The United Methodist Church—open doors, open minds, open . . . " something else—I forgot.

One clergy cynic, after the session, summed up these church ads with, "Self-centered, whining yuppies of the world, have we got a church for you!"[7]

The British homiletician of a previous generation, R. E. C. Browne once noted that there comes a point when the gospel seems to be too little to go on. In such a moment, the temptation for preachers is to go beyond our authority and to rest what we say on grounds other than the promises of God. When we do, says Browne, we succumb to "an atheistic anxiety."[8] It is precisely this "atheistic anxiety" that bothers Willimon about the United Methodist media blitz. Instead of being called to repent and believe in the gospel, the not-so-subtle message of these television spots, he argued, is to indulge your self-centeredness and to do so under the auspices of the very church that, by dent of history and theology, ought to know better.

As a scholar who occasionally teaches preaching as well as practices the art, Willimon is alarmed that even the best preachers and homileticians of our day have unwittingly joined in this vast conspiracy to replace the gospel with self-directed individualism. He is sharply critical, for example, of Fred B. Craddock's *As One Without Authority*, one of the groundbreaking monographs in the recent history of preaching. When Craddock proposes a dynamic, problem-solving method of preaching, which he calls "inductive," and argues that such a method "respects rather than insults the hearer and . . . leaves the freedom and hence the obligation to respond,"[9] Willimon sniffs out that Craddock has borrowed his idea of "freedom" not from Paul but from the

American marketplace. "Freedom [in Craddock] is not the freedom to choose or to reject Christ," complains Willimon,

> or the freedom of all the baptized to wrestle together over the implications of the gospel. Freedom, in *As One Without Authority*, is freedom of the individual, apart from Scripture or community, to draw his or her own democratic conclusions. This is an example of what Alasdair MacIntyre in *After Virtue* calls "emotivism," the primary stance of modern people that renders all other stances subordinate to the sovereign individual.[10]

So, in the light of the trouble he sees in his hearers, and in the face of the vast conspiracy of worldviews and institutions to keep them in trouble, Willimon has no choice but to preach for a bold conversion to the Christian story. At a pastors' conference, Willimon was challenged by a participant who demanded to know whether he really thought Christians ought to try to convert the world. "Absolutely!" he responded. "If you don't want them converted to Christianity, what do you want them converted to?" He went on to explain:

> There is no "world"—self-evident, natural, normal—just sitting out there. Everybody lives somewhere. Everybody is standing somewhere. So . . . when you say, "I don't want to impose my point of view on you, I don't want to convert you to Christianity," what you are really saying is, "I want to leave you alone so that capitalism, consumerism, materialism, and all the ideologies that control this culture can have their way with you. . . . " Why should we Christians do that?[11]

Follow the Leader

We have a sense, then, of what Willimon is against and what forces he thinks he is battling, but what is discipleship, in a positive sense, for him? In a way, the answer is deceptively simple:

Discipleship is following Jesus. Like the apprentice to a master carpenter, a Christian is to imitate the Master, to put his or her feet in the prints made for us by Jesus, to form and conform our lives, our loves, our decisions, our actions as much as we can around the pattern given to us by him. "It is more important to be a disciple, a follower of Jesus, than even to be a Christian," he announced in a sermon. "Christianity is not a set of beliefs, first principles, propositions. It is a matter of discipleship, following. Faith in Jesus is not beliefs about Jesus. It is a willingness to follow Jesus. The faith is in the following."[12]

And why should people follow? Why would they *want* to follow? Willimon does not argue Jesus' case. He does not give fifteen reasons why following Jesus is more attractive, satisfying, or logical than following Wall Street or the secret desires of one's heart. Rather, he gives testimony. He is like an explorer who rushes breathlessly back to camp shouting that he has found the long-sought pass through the mountains. People are motivated to follow Jesus, to obey Jesus' commands, because they trust that this is the way that leads to life. In the same way that a pupil of a master violinist would obey the teacher's commands because the student is persuaded that the master violinist knows the way to excellence, and would obey those commands even if they did not in the moment make sense, just so, a Christian puts one foot in front of the other and follows, even when the way seems hard and the commands seem contrary to reason, because the Christian trusts that Jesus is leading to green pastures. All the way down at bedrock, Christians become disciples, learners, students, followers because of an unwavering conviction about the character of God. "We Christians do not just obey to obey," Willimon writes, "but we obey because the God we worship has been faithful to us. . . . So we often do that which we do not understand, and in the process we become God's church."[13]

Willimon points to baptism, even more specifically to his own baptism, as a picture of what discipleship is all about. He notes that he was baptized as an infant in the living room of his grandmother's South Carolina home. "Someone," he writes, "had to hold me, administer the water of baptism, tell the story of what

Jesus had done and the promise of what he would do, and model the life of faith for me. It was all gift, all grace."[14]

Observe how deeply this runs against the grain of popular American religion. Willimon did not shop around in the market-place of religious ideas for the best buy. He did not hold out for a worldview that made sense or flicked on his inner light. Here at the beginning of his Christian life he was, instead, a passive recipient of a pattern that did not say "make this up as you go along" but "follow me." His baptism was a sign that "becoming a Christian is something done to us and for us before it is anything done by us."[15]

Peculiar Speech

Can Willimon be criticized as a preacher? Of course. Like one of the Flying Wallendas, he has chosen to perform a publicly vis-ible high-wire act, walking the cable across the yawning abyss of culture and always working without a net. He is sometimes big-ger than life; like many a fine preacher before him, he knows the power of hyperbole, and the color contrast on his language is always high. On occasion, he does not wait for God to humble the proud and exalted, but does it himself. He doesn't suffer fools gladly, and if he came across a real live yuppie Zacchaeus up in the tree checking his Rolex to see when the parade was coming by, instead of saying, like Jesus, "I must stay at your house today," he might pummel him with tennis balls instead.

If Willimon can be criticized for sometimes being too brash, he can also be faulted for blunting his message with an overabun-dance of charm. His friend Stanley Hauerwas is reported to have said,

> My main criticism is that Willimon is far too subtle, much too charming. It's that Southern soft-talk thing that he does so well. I keep hoping that one of these days he is going to get the gospel so right and so clear that the university administration will finally figure out what he's talking about and say, "This guy

is against everything we believe! Fire him!" He hasn't yet
preached that well, but I keep hoping.[16]

Perhaps, but when it comes around to Willimon's preaching on
discipleship, my complaint is not that he is too brash or too
charming or, gracious sakes, too southern. Indeed, my criticism is
not that he should do other, but that he should do more. In the
first place, while it is true, as Willimon says, that Jesus does not
meet our needs (at least as we late-modern consumers would
define them), the New Testament does present Jesus as a compelling presence. Fishermen got out of their boats and followed,
sinners drew near, those who had run out of hope clung to his
cloak, and people heard him gladly. I am speaking here more of
what Willimon chooses to emphasize than something lacking in
his preaching. Willimon rightly wants to make sure we know that
the road from Jordan's chilly waters is a road we did not choose
on our own, a road we could not have found for ourselves, and a
road that leads over rough terrain to eternal life. As a Calvinist,
I applaud this in his preaching, but as a Calvinist I also wish there
were more about Jesus as the revelation of the providential God,
the God of great kindness and mercy. I am glad that Willimon
wants us to sing "Must Jesus Bear the Cross Alone." I also want
to sing "Be Thou My Vision" and "I Greet Thee Who My Sure
Redeemer Art." Yes, Jordan's waters are chilly and cold, but the
path from baptism, the way of the cross, leads to the banquet
table where we meet the God of Jesus Christ who gives gift after
gift after gift, and it is not just our "duty" but also our "delight" to
say, "Thank you. Thank you. Thank you."

In the second place, I would like more doctrine in Willimon's
treatment of discipleship. I realize that asking for doctrine in a
sermon sounds like asking for castor oil in a chocolate sundae,
but discipleship cannot finally be sustained without theological
reflection. Willimon is absolutely correct that discipleship is, at
root, picking up one's feet and following Jesus, but this means
more, of course, than putting on a W.W.J.D. bracelet. Trying to
figure out what it means to follow the Galilean in a multicultural,
multifaith, global environment means more than trying to deci-

pher which story of Jesus from the New Testament more or less fits each event of the day. Instead it means trying, in the midst of the Church's ongoing inquiry, to discover what God in Christ is doing today and joining ourselves to God's action. This is a complex process that involves thinking through the Christian faith in a trinitarian framework. Preachers who try this in the pulpit go down in deep water, of course, but the rings on the surface are themselves a witness to the life of discipleship.

Essentially, though, I find myself an admirer of Willimon, the preacher of discipleship. He is a unique gift to the American pulpit in our time. In lesser hands, his calls to come to the cross would be mere nostalgic appeals for a return to a long-lost and best-forgotten tent meeting piety. If he were not so eloquent, he would be dismissed as a pulpit thumper. If he were not so clear-minded and sure-voiced about the demands of the gospel, he could well be viewed benignly as an effete university chaplain who can charm visitors and properly hold a teacup, a liturgical Martha Stewart who knows how to set the sermonic table with lovely words that "go nicely" with the music. But Willimon is a rare combination of the prophet Amos and the preacher Apollos. Like Apollos, he is "an eloquent man, well-versed in the scriptures" (Acts 18:24), but like Amos, he is not afraid to charge into the king's chapel with a brash word of repentance.

Yes, the preacher Willimon can be criticized, and has been many times. But when you see him up there—toeing the wire, the wind of the gospel blowing strong around him, the risks great, the possibility for failure high—and you watch him edge out over the depths, urging all the gawkers below to leave the safety of their boring picnics and dull amusements and to take up the great adventure of the Christian faith, then all criticisms fall mute before awestruck admiration. It's easy down in the gulch to say he should be more this or less that, but watching him up on that thin wire, you realize this takes not only skill but also great courage.

CHAPTER 5

CONVERSION AND TRANSFORMATION: "CHRISTIANS ARE MADE, NOT BORN"

While Journeying, Suddenly a Light from Heaven

ACTS 9:1-6

April 29, 2001

Now as he was going along and approaching Damascus, suddenly a light from heaven flashed around him. He fell to the ground and heard a voice. . . . (Acts 9:3-4)

What a great story, this conversion of Saul. Saul, Church Enemy Number One, murderous persecutor of the Church, is struck down on his way to hunt Christians, blinded by light, name changed. Now his life is so new that he is called Paul, great missionary to the Gentiles.

It is a story always told by the Church in the afterglow of Easter. We're just three Sundays from Easter, that day when the stone was rolled from the tomb, light shown, and the Risen Christ burst the bonds of death.

Well, so what? What if Jesus has been raised from the dead, brought from death to life? So what about us? In answer, the Church tells us the story of how a man named Saul got born again.

95

Over the front door of this chapel, welcoming you, is a statue of John Wesley. His is a story almost as dear to Methodists as the story of the change of Saul to Paul. Wesley was a proper little Oxford don, a priest, a devout Christian who had devoted his life to study and proclamation of the gospel. But he had no fire. After a disastrous stint as missionary in Georgia, he went, in his words "unwillingly," to a meeting in Aldersgate Street in London. There, while someone was reading Luther's rather dull commentary on Paul's Letter to the Romans, Wesley's heart was "strangely warmed." His soul struck fire, and the Wesleyan revival began.

It was, for Wesley, just like Saul on the Damascus road.

Maybe you enjoy stories like these more than I do. I confess that I am of that age when I have come to take inordinate joy in keeping things in their place. Bloom where you are planted, I say. Slippers under the bed, toothbrush always in the same place, everything just as it was yesterday and the day before. Something out of place during my morning rituals of awakening, say, no cornflakes in the box, and I am out of sync for the rest of the day.

So there is something about Paul's Damascus road story that is for me, past fifty, less than appealing.

And I confess to membership in a church of a certain age that loves everything just in the place where it was yesterday and the day before. I go to mainline Protestant church meetings and behold a sea of hair the same color as mine. Wesley's once bub-bling church of revivals, great awakenings, and new birth has become geriatric, the church of the over-fifty crowd. Cement. People on top, people well-fixed, content, self-satisfied, for whom the world has been particularly good, don't need much change, and don't get much. We prefer to set out on a journey, moving deliberately from point A to point B with a minimum of devia-tion, no disruption or dislocation. We are awfully well-accom-modated, well-situated, at ease in Zion, disgustingly content with present arrangements. Oh Lord, we pray, preserve us from big moves.

Can't teach an old dog new tricks; sometimes even a young one is difficult to budge.

Yet deep in our hearts there's this story of a man who got knocked down, blinded by light on the Damascus road, a story that challenges all characterizations of the Christian life as a pleasantly continuous progression from point A to point B with no jerks, jolts, lurches to the left or the right along the way.

But sometimes, by the grace of God, while we're on our way, suddenly a light surprises, God gets to us, grabs us, jerks, jolts, blinds us, and we do change.

Historian Gary Wills says that if you are a white, male, Southerner over fifty (guilty!), there is no way to convince you that people cannot change. Having experienced radical transformation of heart and mind on matters of race, within your own family, deep in your own soul, you are completely convinced of the possibility of radical human alteration.

Writer Anne Braden grew up in the South, the old South, in a privileged family in the 1930s. As a college student, she had dinner one night with an African American woman. There, at the table, sharing a meal together, she was born again. In words worthy of Paul she later wrote, "It was a tremendous revelation, the turning point of my life. All the cramping walls of a lifetime seemed to have come tumbling down in that moment. Some heavy shackles seemed to have fallen from my feet. For the first time in my nineteen years on this earth, I felt I had room to stretch my arms and legs and lift my head high toward the sky. . . . Here for a moment I glimpsed a vision of the world as it should be, where people are people, and spirits have room to grow. I never got over it."[1]

One of the great things about being a pastor is that you have these people stagger in, not every day, but on some days, and they have just been plodding along in life, minding their own business, keeping their heads down, plowing the same furrow, not expecting, not even wanting conversion, and somehow God reaches in, grabs them by the neck, shakes them up and down, and they, despite themselves, are different.

Their stories are a great challenge to the conventional, socially approved atheism of the academy. Though I try, I can find no sociological, economic, gender-determined, psychological explanation for why they are now who they are. After asking them the typical, "As a young child, did your mother beat you?" "Have you recently been dumped by your girlfriend?" "Is there some unresolved grief in your life?" "Have you eaten recently in a Mexican restaurant?" all I can do is say, "Well, I guess then there really is a living God, for how else to explain this sudden lurch to the left in your life?"

Any God who would raise somebody from the dead, and after three days in the tomb, is just the sort of God who would think it cool to jerk someone around at fifty. So C. S. Lewis spoke of his life before conversion as that time "before God closed in on me," and of his conversion, a moment when he was "surprised by joy."

Most of the time I portray the Christian life as a process of orderly progression, spiritual disciplines, faith development: Do this from seven until eight, be here on Sundays from eleven to twelve, now read this, eventually you should get that. But sometimes, by the sheer surprising grace of God, someone gets grabbed, God jumps someone unawares, closes in, claims, converts, calls, like Saul on the Damascus road.

From this pulpit, back in January, Barbara Brown Taylor told of the time she spent on a seminary admissions committee. They turned this student down, a student who obviously had few academic qualifications for theological study. But he wrote them from his jail cell to tell them that the parole board would let him out if they let him in. They invited him to plead his case before them. Barbara described, from this pulpit, how this big guy came in and told them that, as a young teenager, he had held up a convenience store. All he remembered was brandishing this unloaded gun at the clerk, and an off-duty policeman spotted him. Shots rang out. Then, before the oak table of the seminary admissions committee, he pulls up his shirt to show them where the policeman's bullet got him in the gut and went out the other side. "That was my Damascus road, my burning bush!" he exclaimed.

Of course, said Barbara, we didn't want to admit him into seminary. But what could we do? We knew Acts 9! If God could make an apostle out of Saul the murderer, what might God do with a guy with a gun?

It was just the sort of thing that a God who would raise Jesus from the dead might do.

And I said that it is a great joy to hear such stories. It is a joy because, well, down deep, even people past fifty have some part of us that thrills to the notion that we can change. It is a joy because if we don't know a story like Saul on the Damascus road, or somebody who gets radically detoured while minding her own business on Elm Street, then how could Easter be true?

Here's my Damascus road story again. I met him his sophomore year, when he arrived at Duke as a transfer student. He was in the Chapel on most Sundays. One day in the fall, I took him home with me for a sandwich. As we sat there eating, he said, "I want to tell you something about me so you can know me a little better."

"Okay."

"Well, first I was a teenager from hell. I made my folks' lives miserable," he said.

I said that was a not too original story around here.

He continued, "They had me committed to a mental institution when I was sixteen. But I escaped from there, made my way to Chicago, worked as a prostitute on the streets. Got into lots of stuff. One night I rolled this guy, took his wallet and used his American Express card to buy some stuff."

"Wow," I said. "I thought you meant that you got a speeding ticket in high school."

"I told you I was bad," he said. "Anyway, cops got me. I was sent to Joliet prison. That was like entering the depths of hell. This older prisoner took me under his wing to protect me. Every night, before lockdown, he would read a chapter out of the Bible to me, out of the Gospel of Luke. He wasn't too good a reader, so it would take him forever, stumbling over the words and stuff. Well, one night he was reading Luke, about the middle, the stories about the lost sheep, and the prodigal son, and all, and it was like this hand just reached in that cell, grabbed me by the throat, shook me up and down, and said, 'I've got plans for you!' Well, I got saved. I got out of that prison in a few months, finished my high school degree, and I'm here on a full scholarship."

"Wow," I said. "We don't hear stories like that around here too often."

"Well," he continued, "the reason I'm telling you this is that you're a preacher, right? And I know you guys are always grubbing around for stories, illustrations and stuff. And you got Easter coming up in a few weeks. Well, I am your proof of Easter."

New World, New You

2 CORINTHIANS 5:16-21

March 25, 2001

This is just me, but I think one of the reasons for the appeal of George W. Bush was his biography. Mr. Bush survived the revelation of his claim "I have changed. I have learned from my youthful indiscretions, and I'm a better person for it."

We like that. Something in all of us is deeply attracted to a person who has changed. We all, in our better moments, long to be somebody better than who we are.

Consider all the self-help books. Nobody ever went broke publishing a book on how to diet or how to change. The irony is that any book on self-help is a lie. If our help were exclusively in ourselves, then why the heck must we pay $19.95 plus postage for somebody else's book in order to help ourselves!

No. The self cannot be the source of our help. The self is the problem, not the solution. The self finds it impossible to will itself a new self. Augustine showed us, better than Freud, that the self has *not* the ability to transform itself. It's a problem of desire. How on earth do we transform desire?

I believe Augustine would agree with me that it's not been a good thing that our culture has conditioned us to think so highly of sex, to feel no guilt over our unbridled sexual desires, to look upon unfettered sexual expression as a right, even a duty. Augustine was not so much against sex as he was fascinated by the way our sexuality is, for most of us, our first real revelation of just how out of control we are, how inept we are to manage our appetites and desires. The brain makes resolutions, decisions, and vows, but then much lesser organs take over. Augustine wondered how in the world he was supposed to save himself by his will when he couldn't even control himself in front of a junior high classroom.

This condition makes all the more remarkable Paul's sweeping claim for the transforming, life-changing power of Christ. To the often wild and wanton Corinthians, Paul preaches, "If anyone is in Christ, there is a new creation." "From now on," he says (i.e., now that Christ has come), "nobody ought to regard us through the categories of the old world." In Christ, it's like God started all over with Genesis 1 and made a new world. There was the first Creation, with God bringing forth light out of darkness and creating all the world. Now, Paul claims, in Christ, it's Genesis 1 all over again.

Richard Hays first pointed out to me the difference between the way our Bibles used to translate this verse: "If any one is in Christ, he is a new creation" (RSV), and the more accurate, "If anyone is in Christ, there is a new creation" (NRSV). Hear the difference? We're not talking about some inner, subjective change of heart in the individual: "If anyone is in Christ, then that person feels differently about things." Paul is saying, "If anyone is in Christ, there is a new creation," *a whole new world.*

"In the beginning, when God began creating the heavens and the earth," begins Genesis. "In the beginning was the Word and the Word was with God and the Word was God. . . . There was not anything made that was made except through him," begins John's Gospel. See what John is doing? The birth of Christ, the Incarnation, is just like a new Creation, new beginning, new world.

Ezekiel was shown a valley full of old, dead, dry bones. "Can these bones live?" Ezekiel is asked. God only knows. God only. There is a breath, a holy wind, just like the wind that brooded over the waters at Creation, and the bones take on life and flesh, stand up, and live. No newness except as a gift of God. God never gets done with creation.

When I was in the sixth grade, we had a boy join our class. He was from Poland, a "displaced person," the teacher told us. Of course, he had terrible problems adjusting to his new home, all the way from devastated Poland to 1950s South Carolina. One of his problems was that he stole food. Although he had plenty of food in his lunch sack, provided by his new American family, out of habit, he would purloin this or that out of our lunch sacks and stuff it in his backpack. Our teacher told him that was not to be done. But he still stole food. One day, our teacher, in exasperation grabbed him by the shoulders and shouted, "Look at me! You don't need to steal food! This is America. There's enough here. I promise you, here, you'll never be hungry again."

And I think then it dawned on him. I could see it in his eyes. He wasn't back in Poland. He was living in a whole new world. His behavior suddenly seemed to him so out of step, so odd, because it was from another, old world, not the one he was in now. I think Paul is talking about something like that. A new world requires a new you.

When her beloved husband died, her world ended. In one skip of a heartbeat, she was no longer a wife, a lover, a friend; she was alone. Yet in the days that followed, she slowly came to realize that it wasn't only that a world, her world, had ended. It was that a new world had begun. Sure, it might not have been the world she would have chosen, but it's usually not up to us to choose our world. Our world is a reality in which we must live or else appear stupidly out of step. Gradually, she realized that she was now living in a new world where she must find a new way of life. I think Paul is talking about something like that.

Paul is talking not primarily about a change in heart, some subjective alteration of feeling. Paul is talking about a whole new world—New Creation. Christ is not something that happened in us; he is something that has happened to us.

My favorite painting of the Renaissance is Piero della Francesca's *Resurrection*. Out of the tomb rises the resurrected Christ, with battle flag and biceps like a fullback. And behind him, on his left, the world is in winter, dead and dry. But there's a faint light on the horizon. And to his right, trees are in full leaf and it is spring, a whole new world. Easter, implies the painter, wasn't just something that happened once to Christ; it is a shifting of the world on its axis, dawn of the first day, New Creation.

When she faced her attacker in court, she told him, in front of the judge, the jury, and everybody, how his attack on her had damaged her forever, caused her unspeakable pain. Then in front of God and everybody, she forgave him. Just stood right there and said, "I forgive."

Now in the aftermath, some said she was an incredibly sweet person anyway, some said she was more than a bit idealistic to behave thus.

She prefers to call what she did "realistic." That is, she really believes that forgiveness is really the way the world works. She believes that forgiveness is built into the grain of the universe. Why? Because when it came time for Jesus to reveal what's what, who God is, how the world is put together, from the cross he said, "Father, forgive." Her behavior was thus in conformity to the facts.

Some people think that Christians live in certain ways—showing compassion for the poor, fidelity in marriage, honesty in relationships, peacefulness and patience—because we are trying to get somewhere with God. We must work hard to keep our slates clean in order to please God. No. Christians live as they live, not to get somewhere, but rather because they know that, in Christ, we've already arrived at a whole new world. To live otherwise would be to appear bafflingly out of step. It would be the equivalent of taking up residence in Turin and yet persisting as if one were still in Tupelo.

That's why a colleague of mine at the Divinity School claims that the best preparation for being a pastor today is to have taught high school French. The same skills of vocabulary inculcation, habit, imitation, and a willingness to move from where you are presently living, linguistically speaking, that will get you an A in French are required to succeed at Christian discipleship. And one reason you take the trouble to learn French is not just so you will know some elaborate words for everyday English objects, but because in learning the language your citizenship is being transferred to a whole new world.

That's why, for Christians, worship is prior to ethics. What we do here on Sunday is of great ethical significance. We get you in here and—in the music, the speaking, reading, processing, eating, and drinking—we try to get you to face facts, to wake up to a whole new world. We don't primarily tell you how to live; we try to get you to see *where* you live. New Creation. If we can get you to change your address, the behavior will take care of itself. You'll know how to act, when you know where you live.

Wake up. Smell the reality. Get in step with Jesus' beat. Welcome to a whole new world.

Conversion and Transformation: "Christians Are Made, Not Born"

Marva J. Dawn

Reading Will Willimon's sermons always makes me wish that I could have been there—sitting among the Duke University students and chatting with them afterward about their new insights into faith. Willimon's language is exhilarating and energizing and, it seems to me (who could be the students' aging aunt), truly in tune with their generation.

In speaking as he does, Willimon demonstrates the validity of his instructions to preachers to begin, as did the apostle Paul at Athens, with the hearers' language, with public speech.[2]

But Paul and Willimon don't stop there. They channel common language into the peculiar language of the new creation, to enfold listeners (especially university students) in the world the Triune God's people inhabit. As Willimon repeatedly stresses in his writings, "Words Make Worlds."[3]

Willimon cites (and follows) Lesslie Newbigin's three-part missionary pattern of speaking the language of the "receptor culture," of *radically* calling "into question that culture's understanding of reality," and of receiving the miracles of God, who uses the missionary's faithfulness to bring listeners to repentance and conversion.[4] Elsewhere, he adds that the purpose of the prophetic ministry of preaching is not merely to criticize current social con-ditions, but to form a peculiar community of people, all empowered to be prophetic.[5] These four dimensions of the preacher's method are amply illustrated in Willimon's sermons.

In his Duke University Chapel addresses, we can hear the cadences of collegians' speech; we can tell that Willimon knows university students and their habits, concerns, and idioms. We can also recognize that he is immersed in, and speaks from, the culture of the gospel, which calls the world as we know it into question. Thereby he enables his listeners, also, prophetically to question their surroundings in light of the alternative narrative of God's kingdom. Above all, Willimon faithfully acclaims the prior invitation and work in us of the Trinity, to which we respond with lives that give God glory.

It's a Great Thing to Hear a "Good Methodist" Preach!

Will Willimon is definitely a follower of John Wesley (not all Methodists are)! That is exceedingly good for the rest of us because he knows he is "not free not to attempt to be faithful to the conversionist and sanctificationist treasure that has been given to us," that to be uniquely Wesleyan is to "*do justice to both ... the radical experience of the new birth and the morally transformative process of growth into Christ.*"[6] He recognizes that there are moments "on the Damascus road" when God "grabs us," as the first sermon in this section declares, but Willimon doesn't stop there, for once we are turned, as the second sermon insists, we have to keep remembering "where we live."

Christianity becomes terribly strenuous (downright impossible) if we have never been grabbed, but keep trying to grab on to spiritual things ourselves. But it gets downright wimpy if we confine God's actions in our lives to the initial call and don't comprehend how thoroughly God enjoys drastic upheaval of all the idolatries and ideologies not in keeping with where we live.

Willimon preaches and writes to help his listeners and readers avoid these opposite dangers of sloth and legalism (trying to manufacture by our own rules what God wants to do in and through us by grace). He reminds us, as did Wesley, of "the triumph of grace, the power of grace to make us that which our earnest efforts could not . . . [namely,] more holy. Sanctification is a work of God in us, a movement from heaven, a light not of our devising."[7]

Other sections in this book have highlighted Willimon's emphasis on radical Christianity and discipleship. It remains for us in this chapter to narrate how Willimon accentuates the source of both conversion and transformation, for it is, after all, "about God, not you," the preacher. It is crucial that we remember—in all our preaching preparations and actual proclamation—that it is God who makes Christians, not we.

The Basic Theology of Willimon's Sermons

We probably all chuckled as we read Michael Turner's summary of Willimon's preaching in chapter 1:

> (1) "God is large, mysterious, and there is no way I could explain it to someone like you," (2) "Life is a mess, and there is no way that I could explain it to someone like you," and (3) "Christianity is weird, odd, peculiar; I can't believe you people actually want to be Christians."[8]

Those themes have, no doubt, been obvious to you in the sermons included in this book. Most of Willimon's sermons contain pieces of all three elements.

Perhaps, however, Willimon himself would add another theme to those three, lest we turn the third element into a Messiah complex on our part to make "better Christians." He might add this as the fourth theme: "Watch out! If you listen enough to the words of this community, you will discover yourself inhabiting that weird Christian new creation!" I suggest this because he skillfully balances the Wesleyan dialectic—that God is the one who converts and transforms, but also that listening to the preached Word; participating in all the elements of worship, including the Sacraments; and practicing other spiritual disciplines are means that God uses to do that metamorphosing work.

Willimon expounds this dialectic well in his concluding chapter to the book *Conversion in the Wesleyan Tradition.* There he emphasizes that conversion leads to a lifetime of daily cross bearing, that "the Christian faith takes time, a lifetime, to get right." Citing Calvin, Willimon cautions that "sin is so deeply rooted in our thinking and willing that only a lifetime of turnings, of fits and starts, of divine dislodgement and detoxification can produce what God has in mind for us."[9]

Never does Willimon lose the sense that it is God who dislodges us, who accomplishes the turnings in us. He summarizes, "Conversion, regeneration, mystical union, and *metanoia* are all attempts to speak of this turning of heart, body, and mind toward God, a turning that is occasioned by God's prior turning toward us in Christ." And again, "Conversion is one of God's most gracious, intrusive, demanding, sovereign acts. '*By his great mercy* he has given us a new birth into a living hope'" (1 Peter 1:3*b*, Willimon's italics).[10]

In one sermon almost chosen for inclusion in this section, Willimon elaborates the meaning of the word *evangel* as "good news"—"It is *news*, something that comes to us, rather than something derived from us. It is *good* because it is something that God does before it is anything we do."

That sermon continues by criticizing our "limp theology of Good News," our failure to learn from Luther the importance of the "external word," that which comes "from the outside, that which is more than we could have contrived ourselves." He emphasizes that we hear "something we would not have known had not the church told us."[11]

This last sentence highlights another significant dimension of Willimon's theology suggested in my #4—that the Good News both creates, and is passed on by, an entire community of people being continually transformed by its power. As he affirms in *Good News in Exile,* the Church provides the setting in which we hear and practice the words of faith, in which we "try them on for size." Christianity requires, as do all communities (such as baseball), that we "take the time, the trouble, to submit to the words and the habits of the different culture."[12]

Now, having underscored Willimon's essential method and theology, let us consider its enfleshment in the two sermons of this section.

A Sermon on Conversion Leading to Transformation

The Sermon's Basic Structure and Willimon's Strengths

Will Willimon's sermon "While Journeying, Suddenly a Light from Heaven" begins with two great paragraphs inviting our immediate interest. Here is that trademark exuberance, Willimon's genuine delight in the stories he tells. These stories of Saul refashioned to Paul, of Christ bursting the bonds of death, are Good News worth talking about. This is the first major theme pointed out by Turner in chapter 1: the magnificence of God and God's Good News.

The sermon's third paragraph, then, urgently presses a critical question for university students: What does all this have to do with us? We've got grades to get, jobs to prepare for, people to impress, all the pressures of university life weighing on us.

Willimon elaborates this question with an impressive paragraph about the church that loves everything to be in place, always the same—a church of self-satisfied cement. Here's a problem with which everyone can identify (though perhaps not with the "over-fifty crowd"). This is the second Turner theme: Life is a mess, in this case because we so dislike change.

Several paragraphs later, Willimon gives a further example, a lovely confession by Anne Braden, who identifies herself as cemented in the privileged old South's perspectives on race until a startlingly liberating conversion refashioned her. This is a perfect story to demonstrate how the magnificent God (theme one) does something about the mess we're in (theme two).

This is the gift of conversion, which Willimon highlights with the stirring sentence: "Sometimes, by the sheer surprising grace of God, someone gets grabbed, God jumps someone unawares, closes in, claims, converts, calls, like Saul on the Damascus road." The sermon amplifies that grace with two other compelling narratives that stretch us to consider similar converting moments in our own experience.

Thus Willimon emphasizes God as the actor, lest we try to manufacture our own conversions. The theme rings out clearly throughout the "While Journeying" sermon. Its narratives of conversion are "proof of Easter."

The Sermon Development and Postmodern Randomness

The powerful movement just outlined demonstrates the conversion-sanctificationist theology that Willimon delineates in his chapter on Wesleyanism. In rebuke of a Methodism "that has lost its conversionist roots, having settled comfortably into a characterization of the Christian life as continuous and synonymous with being a good person," he sketches the "rich array of metaphors" in the Scriptures that "speak of the discontinuous, discordant outbreak of new life." Furthermore, this new life is not merely subjective experience, for, as the story of Paul on the Damascus road demonstrates, those whom God so shakes are transferred into, and transformed by, a whole new world.[13]

I am forever grateful for Will Willimon's theology and for the power of his preaching as it has influenced thousands of students and preachers. But one of his weaknesses, his frequent lack of clear organization, raises serious questions.

Is this style beneficial for university students? Though many of Willimon's sermons seem to be produced by a scattergun, his ideas and insights are superb (though sometimes not logically ordered). Of the several sermons suggested by this book's editors, I chose to include in this section the two that were the best organized, but even in these two the thoughts sometimes seem to jump around too fast.

Such a style perhaps is appropriate in an increasingly post-modern society typically characterized by such randomness. University students are accustomed to watching news programs in which three or four things are happening at the same time on various sections of the screen. They have habits of Web surfing that splash from site to site, with barely a toe-dabble in each ocean of information. They like to carry on several conversations at once—one with their companions, others on their mobile phones and palm computers, and perhaps a continuing one in their own souls.

But the question is this: What kind of formation can ensue? Is a montage of good ideas dispersed in jumbled order the best way to build the kind of community in which believers can practice the language of faith—even if that is the most appealing kind of discourse for those who hear?

We can't answer these questions. None of us can actually measure the effectiveness of Willimon's sermons. We know that the Holy Spirit blesses them for God's purposes, for countless students have found Duke Chapel substantially consequential for their faith, and we who write this book acknowledge our debts to Willimon.

Those of us deeply ingrained by patterns of linear thought can't rightly judge whether younger people can actually pay attention to four or five simultaneous things or to bits of information heard in clumps not necessarily connected together. I can only urge in this essay that those mentored by Willimon's teaching and preaching should continually ask themselves whether more time invested in creating logical progressions of thought would detract from the vivacity and allure of one's sermons or whether the time apportioned for the sake of clarity in both sequence and illustration would produce more thorough and lasting results.

For example, the sermon "While Journeying" includes these fits and starts among others: The third paragraph ends by asserting that the Church tells the story of Saul to answer our question "So what?" but then the next sentence talks about John Wesley. Several paragraphs later Willimon says that he finds such stories as those of Wesley and Saul less than appealing—but he later names as one of the "great things about being a pastor" that he gets to hear such stories! The third paragraph says that the Church tells the story of Saul getting born again to answer the question of what the resurrection of Jesus has to do with us, but Willimon doesn't really tell us that story at all.

These discrepancies are listed not because I want to nitpick a great preacher. That is the occupation of someone who wants to prove he or she is better, which, of course, I'm not. I know I can only be a second-rate preacher, since as a guest I do not know the congregation well enough for that community to preach through and with me by means of my long-term prayer for, and daily interaction with, the people individually and corporately. Will Willimon is a great preacher because he knows his students, loves them deeply, and regularly practices the language of faith with them.

I list these incongruities instead to ask whether sometimes Willimon's very worthwhile intentions for his sermons are thwarted by lack of clarity in purpose and progression. If they are, Willimon would be the first to know that his weaknesses are not only forgiven, but also overcome by the Holy Spirit's power. He would also be the first to want his mentorees not to follow him in less-than-the-best habits.

But the jury is still out. Has there been any conclusive research on extended effects of less logically developed sermons on the formation of individual Christian character and corporate community life? Who could ever know the prolonged consequences of God's habitation in the words of such a faithful preacher?

I raise these questions in the hope that they'll stay raised. Each of us who preaches must ever ask God for guidance in the proportioning of our time spent for structuring sermons—especially in conjunction with our other tasks and our relationships with the communities we serve—for the sake of offering our best for God to use in sanctifying Christians and building communities.

My own structuring is most often given by the text itself because I generally preach on a larger (usually narrative) section of Scripture, whereas Willimon seems typically to use one verse or two. The disadvantage of my approach is that longer texts say far too much; the advantage of Willimon's is that he can present to his listeners one major point thoroughly illustrated and illuminated.

The Sermon's Goal and Tying Up Loose Ends

Reading sermons gives us the advantage of rereading. Consequently, when Willimon says toward the end of the sermon that "down deep, even people past fifty have some part of us that thrills to the notion that we can change," we can finally put together his first-page dislike of conversion stories with his second-page declaration that as a pastor he likes to hear them.

Perhaps the initially jarring contradiction is an intentional, useful device for accentuating the sermon's goal, to prove Easter by our own startling experiences of Damascus road conversions. Certainly Willimon's final story in the "While Journeying" sermon is a poignant narration that stirs us into remembering our own moments of being blinded by truth.

Surely one of Willimon's best gifts is his robust sense of story. Faith is not passed on so much by analysis or doctrinal definition (secondary speech at best), but by narration that invites participation. I can't imagine students leaving Duke Chapel after this sermon without pondering their own (or lack of) resurrections.

In an age when many people are starved for hope, Willimon constantly offers it. God is always at work, grabbing us, shedding light, turning us around. If we keep hanging around Duke Chapel enough, we will learn this Christian language and will discover ourselves inhabiting the Triune God's new creation!

A Sermon on Transformation and the New Creation

Problems, Solutions, and Sermonic Intensification

In the sermon "New World, New You," Willimon thoroughly states the problem with which his remarks will deal and intensifies our awareness of the mess life is. In doing so, he vigorously demonstrates that God is our only hope.

This is a crucial point in which all of us who preach need to be mentored. Our listeners don't need more self-help sermons, for, as Willimon reveals in his exposure of the deception of self-help books, the self can't "will itself a new self." His brilliant decision to let sexuality, one of the most prominent issues for university students, illustrate how "out of control we are" intensifies our longing for some sort of escape into new life.

Then, what Good News it is that "in Christ, it's like God started all over with Genesis 1 and made a new world." Next, Willimon reinforces our hope by citing the newer translation of 2 Corinthians 5:17, which properly names not merely an inner individual change, but the breakthrough of *"a whole new world."* Successive examples from John's Gospel, and Ezekiel, and his childhood Polish friend continue to add fuel to the flame of desire already kindled.

How Much Scripture Do the Listeners Know?

Willimon's references to Genesis and John and Ezekiel raise the important issue of how much his sermons equip listeners with biblical knowledge so that scriptural language can actually shape their character individually and corporately. On the positive side, Willimon himself unquestionably knows that the sermon is just one piece of an entire worship service, and worship is one practice of many in the Christian community that imbue us with the language of the Word.[14]

Furthermore, Willimon's sermons usually include scattered references to verses other than the primary one that his comments are meant to illustrate. For example, another sermon considered for this chapter, which he delivered in a Parents' Weekend in 2000, gave some orientation to the fourth commandment to honor parents in the context of the Ten Commandments and cited a few instances of Jesus' commands and deeds regarding parents.

However, on the negative side, Willimon's sermons don't actually use very much of the Scriptures. Not much attention is paid to orienting the listeners to the context of the verses cited, to giving extended attention to any one text, to framing the text by its place in the whole meta-narrative of the Scriptures.

How much Scripture do the listeners actually learn? How able are they to recognize the verses Willimon cites because of larger familiarities with texts or to place the verses soundly into their vocabulary because the verses have been connected to the entire web of their biblical knowledge?

Again, we can't answer these questions since we're not able to judge the effectiveness of Willimon's sermons. The questions are important for each of us, however, because the Word is a major means the Holy Spirit uses to form us as people of faith. Therefore, we all need to keep wrestling with how best to invite our listeners into the vocabulary and to train them in well-grounded biblical speech and life.

More deeply, as Willimon himself reminds us in *Pastor* with an illustration from Augustine, we who preach must remember that "ordinary fidelity to the Word enables us to speak the right word in due season in a prophetic, truthful way. By being securely attached to the Scriptures, by desiring to honor the saints in our pastoral work, we become the prophetic pastors we are meant to be."[15] Our own practices of personal Bible study are crucial to form us in the language and world of faith, so that our sermons pulse with new creation life.

Teaching Methods and Learning Results

Education professors in my college days emphasized that we should tell students what we're going to teach, teach, and then remind them of what we've taught. Such a method offers students clear instruction about what is most important. Its disadvantage is that many stories best make their point without any review of "what they mean," since a narrative always means more than its summary.

In general, Willimon wisely senses the subtle difference between nudging a point to make it more memorable and hammering a summary that spoils the story. A good instance is provided in this "New World" sermon by the luminous sentence that ends the story of his Polish classmate, "A new world requires a new you."

Perhaps its punch is spoiled a bit by the jerky move to a new story—a move we can't quite catch because of the ambiguous pronoun *her* two words later. In fact, the next several stories suddenly begin without any hints to prepare us to change subjects. This problem, however, occurs only on the printed page; in a live sermon the transitions to new stories are made with voice inflections and pauses. We each must consider how best to help our listeners move with us when we shift topics in our own sermons.

The last three paragraphs of the sermon pose another problem, for they introduce two different subjects—that of learning the Christian language and that of the relationship of worship and ethics. Possibly Willimon intended to introduce these topics to whet the students' appetites for a future, more thorough elaboration. Most of the people reading this book have also read his discussions of these themes in other places, so we understand what he means by these brief paragraphs, but Sunday worshipers might find the move toward the sermon's ending a bit too abrupt.

Whether it is too abrupt depends partly on what is Willimon's final goal. The last sentence of the second to last paragraph would be a great conclusion: "You'll know how to act when you know where you live." In that case, the sermon's ultimate goal would be to talk about the "New You."

Willimon, however, adds another paragraph, which concludes instead with an emphasis on the "New World." It might be the fault of my whole orientation toward linear progressions, but the last paragraph seems to me a bit anticlimactic. The sermon's whole propelling movement from the "New World" to the "New You" might have been more forcefully concluded with a closing paragraph something like this: "Wake up. There's been a New Creation. Welcome to a whole new world. You'll know how to act when you know where you live."

Feel free to disagree. Actually the only point I want to make is that we who preach must plan carefully how we will conclude our sermons, so that any culminating summary will precisely remind the listeners of what they have learned and end with what we want to end.

Concluding Theological Plaudits

In the chapter discussing the relation of the Church and the world in *Where Resident Aliens Live*, Willimon and his friend Stanley Hauerwas describe what happens in Sunday worship as "a clash of narratives."[16] By means of the entire worship service—and particularly the sermon—participants gain a new eschatological perspective on the world in which we live, a vista that enables them to recognize their location in the midst of unseen, hope-full realities. Rightly knowing their address in this "New World," worshipers then gradually find themselves changed into a "New You"—by the grace and power of the Triune God.

Later in the same chapter, the authors call Christians to disciplined participation in the truth and mission of the faith, guided by pastoral leaders "who have the courage and humility to remind the church of those practices necessary for us to be in unity with God, with one another, and with the church universal."[17] William Willimon is a great model of, and mentor in, such courage and humility. Thanks be to God!

PART II

BROADER ESSAYS

CHAPTER 6

EXPLAINING WHY WILL WILLIMON NEVER EXPLAINS

Stanley Hauerwas

Blowing Willimon's Cover

Will Willimon is one of the least obvious people I have ever known. He is very good at being less than obvious. He appears to be such a nice guy. He wants everyone to like him. He has self-irony down to a fine art. Indeed I think Will is one of the best practitioners of the "Southern Con" I have ever known. The Southern Con is usually perfected by Southerners who have had to live for a time in that mythic place called "The North." I do not know if Will perfected his use of the Southern Con while he was at Yale, but he is a paradigmatic example of this extremely useful strategy.

The Southern Con can take many different forms, but there is a common structure to the way it works. It goes something like this: "I'm just a good ol' boy from the red dirt of South Carolina so I don't have your sophistication. Indeed I am not even sure I know what the word *sophistication* means. But if I heard you right it seems to me that . . ." The dots represent the Southern Con artist's use of a quote from Plato or Dylan Thomas that subverts their interlocutor's position. Of course they pretend they do not know it is a quote from Plato or Dylan Thomas, but you better believe they know what they are doing when they express their "ignorance." Southerners secretly suspect that Paul must have had some proleptic training in being a Southerner, because his speech to the Athenians in Acts 17 is a paradigmatic example of the Southern Con.

Even though I am not from "The South" (Texans simply do not have the passive-aggressive tendencies Southerners confuse with charm), I admire Will's use of the Southern Con. He uses the strategy of the Southern Con to hide his extraordinary reading habits as well as his intellectual depth. Will Willimon—no matter how many times he tells you he is just another Methodist preacher—is an exceptionally smart guy. I will use this occasion, therefore, to expose the metaphysical presumptions that inform Will's preaching and his understanding of pastoral theology.[1] I will explain why Will never explains, and why his refusal to provide explanations is so important for those who would and should imitate him.

Before I take up the task of explaining why Will never explains, however, I need to call attention to some of the other less than obvious aspects of Will's character and work. One of the aspects of Will's life that can be missed is his extraordinary love of The United Methodist Church. I could not understand, for example, why Will would have ever "wanted" to be a bishop. I counseled him not to let his name go forward. I pointed out that if he was elected bishop, he would have to spend the rest of his life dealing with mediocre guys who expressed their frustration with the ministry by sleeping with the wrong person, but he was undeterred. There is, I think, only one explanation for his willingness to go through the demeaning exercise called "electing a bishop": Will really loves The United Methodist Church. One of the things that I love about Will is that he not only loves the Methodist church, but he loves the differences he often finds in and between the denominations before whom he speaks. Will is a critic of the Church, but his criticisms are those only a lover could produce.

Will is also quite adept at hiding the fact he is intellectual. He loves ideas. He seems so "people-orientated" and "pastoral," but I know of few people who read as much as Will. He not only loves to read, but he loves to read in areas about which he knows almost nothing. That means Will is not an academic. He is far too undisciplined (and I mean the description "undisciplined" to be a compliment) to be an academic. That is the reason he is such a good dean of the Chapel at Duke. There is almost nothing in which he is not interested. As a result his sermons, and his books, are filled with wonderful surprises—surprises that make hearing and reading him such a pleasure.

Finally I think it is not at all obvious that Will, as the title of this book suggests, is a prophet. Will may be a prophet, even a "peculiar prophet," but I suspect that description embarrasses him. I am often introduced as a prophet, and I know I am embarrassed to be so described. No one making as much money as Will and I make, as compromised by our positions in the contemporary university as we are, as culturally accommodated as we are, should be described as a prophet. We both get too much pleasure out of what we do to be so described. Prophets usually have to be forced to be prophets. Prophets do not find their calling fun. Yet Will is filled with fun, which is one of the attractive aspects of his ministry. At the very least prophets are usually only rightly identified retrospectively.

I make this observation about Will as a prophet to suggest that one of the other less obvious aspects of Will's character is that he is genuinely modest. He is so, I suspect, because he is constantly surprised that he is getting away with what he is getting away with. I recognize his surprise, because I look upon my own life in quite similar fashion. Will and I do not come from "high cotton" families or cultures. We live in fear that someone will stand up after we have spoken and ask, "You really do not know what you are talking about, do you?" We will have to acknowledge that we really do not know what we are talking about, but we are determined to say what we think necessary anyway. Will is determined to say what he thinks needs to be said because he is possessed by a passion for the gospel. Yet, the same passion that makes him go where only fools would go also makes Will modest. How could it be otherwise, given the gospel he must preach week after week?

I hope that in these few remarks about Will's character I have "blown his cover." He is one of the least obvious people I have ever known. That has everything to do with why he is rightly seen as one of our best preachers. He is not conned by his own use of the Southern Con, which means his sermons and his pastoral theology display an honesty that we desperately need. I have no doubt that is why so many look to him as an exemplary preacher and pastor.

Why Willimon Never Explains

Will Willimon has less philosophical ability than anyone I have ever met. Will likes to tell the story that in his first course in philosophy in college the instructor asked him to sit in the back of the room and, in effect, color in his coloring book. The instructor did so after Will had tried day in and day out to ask questions. There is just something about philosophy that Will does not get. I do not mean it to be a compliment that he does not "get philosophy," but I do think his lack of philosophical ability is one of the reasons he is such a good preacher. Let me explain why Will does not explain.

One of the remarkable things about Will's sermons is he does not try to help us understand what is "really going on" in the text. He does not try to explain the passage from Scripture because he does not think the text is really about "something else." In other words, he does not assume that there is a depth we need to discover that is more important than the text itself. The assumption by many that such a depth is there or needs to be there is often the result of philosophical training of which Will is happily innocent. Some of us were only able to get over our philosophical hunger for "depth" through the extensive therapy provided by Wittgenstein. Since Will had never been seduced by prior philosophical commitments—more specifically, the need for a "theory"—he did not need Wittgenstein.

At least during the time I have been listening to Will's sermons, he has never invited his hearers to find something more basic or important than the stories we find in the Scripture. Some of his most memorable sermons are those with one- or two-word titles such as "More," "Here," or his memorable Easter sermon, "He's Back."[2] In those sermons, Willimon works to free us from our narcissistic desire to find some deeper meaning in the text, something relevant to our lives. He reminds us that the "meaning" of the text is that it helps us understand anything at all about a God who would show up as Jesus.

Let me try to illustrate how I think Willimon works by providing an example I often use. When I was in seminary I saw the film *The Servant*, which featured the great English actor Dirk Bogarde. The film tells the story of the second son of an entitled and wealthy British family. The son has come back to England after serving in the army in India. (Second sons had to serve in the army because they were second sons.) The film takes place in England some time in the early twentieth century at the height of British imperial power. Returning home, the young man realizes he needs "a man servant," because he is, after all, from the English upper classes and accordingly has no sense of how to get through life. Dirk Bogarde plays the servant who is hired to help this young man reintegrate himself into upper-class society.

Bogarde does all that is expected, teaching his master what clothes to wear, what club he ought to join, who his friends should be, what to eat at a restaurant. The young man quickly becomes quite a success. In the process of helping his master become a "gentleman," however, the servant introduces the young man to gambling, the use of drugs, and the use of women who are willing to sell sexual favors to men. The servant does so because such behaviors are activities in which unattached English gentlemen are thought to engage. By the end of the movie, however, the young man squanders his wealth, becomes a hopeless drug addict, and is arrested for killing a woman he had been involved with sexually. In the last scene of the movie, in

which his master is arrested, the servant—whom we now understand has planned the destruction of the one he serves from the
beginning—simply walks away.

What is fascinating about this movie is that no explanation is
given for the servant's project of destroying his master. No sug-
gestions about the servant's motivations are made in the movie.
You simply watch the servant leading the young man to his
destruction. Leaving the theater (I have seen the film several
times), you hear people say to one another, "proletarian revenge"
or a "clear case of repressed homosexuality." The film leaves you
desperate for an explanation. But it gives you no explanation, so
the viewer must supply one. Yet I think the film is trying to suggest that this is exactly what you should not do, because there is
no explanation for evil.

Often I have used this example to suggest to my students why
the "story of the fall" in the book of Genesis takes the form of a
story. The story does not explain how sin came into the world.
The story cannot explain how sin came into the world, because
there can be no explanation for why sin came into the world. Sin
should not exist, but it does. Barth rightly calls sin an ontologi-
cal impossibility in order to indicate that sin is, quite simply,
absurd.[3] Indeed it is a mistake to think that the description "sin"
explains human evil. Sin is not an explanation of something
deeper. Instead, given the story of the Bible, sin names that for
which no other description will do.

In like manner, the language of "creation" does not explain our
existence. Rather that language is a description required by our
faith to remind us that we are created. To ask why there is something rather than nothing may be an interesting exercise for the
philosophically minded. I suspect, however, those that seek to use
the question to try to convince others they must believe in a god
because "something must have started it all" is a mistake. God is
not an explanation for our existence. Rather God is the name
given to us to address the One alone who is worthy of worship.
That Christians believe God is the Father, Son, and Holy Spirit
is but the discovery of the Church, which is made possible and
necessary by the death and resurrection of Christ and the work of

the Spirit at Pentecost. However, we are not explaining God when we learn to address God as Trinity.

I believe nothing more characterizes Will's preaching than his respect for the language, the vocabulary, of the faith as a grammar of description. His sermons are the ongoing attempt to help himself and his hearers learn the grammar of the faith by learning to recognize when they have said all that can be said. I have no idea from whom or how Willimon learned to so preach, but I certainly think all the reading he has done in Barth over the years could not have hurt. The very character of Barth's *Dogmatics* is shaped by his fundamental conviction that you cannot explain the Christian faith. Attempts to "explain" are just another name for the failed project of Protestant liberalism. Barth left explanation behind because he recognized that if God is God then we cannot explain who God is on any grounds other than divine self-revelation.

Barth quite wonderfully imitates the character of the Bible by refusing to say more than can be said. I think the irresistible temptation for some to try to write "a life of Jesus" is fueled by the Gospels' reticence to elaborate on Jesus' life. We want to know more about Jesus' childhood. But we are told so little. "And Jesus increased in wisdom and in years, and in divine and human favor" (Luke 2:52). That is all we are going to get. The Gnostic gospels, however, cannot resist telling us more about his childhood and, of course, that is why they are Gnostic gospels. Gnosticism in its many forms is but the temptation to know more than is needed.

Will's sermons are his way of trying to help us resist the temptation to explain. We are not to speculate about what "must have really been going on" in Jesus' self-consciousness. Attempts to discern what Jesus must have been thinking in this or that circumstance fail to be disciplined by the silence of Scripture. Not only do attempts to "figure Jesus out" presuppose a quite misleading philosophical psychology, but they are sinful just to the extent that such attempts represent our attempt to make the gospel fulfill our desires. The "search for the historical Jesus," I fear, is too often but a symptom of our pride: a pride, moreover, that refuses to be humbled by the invitation to be a disciple. We try to substitute "trying to understand" for following Jesus and all the difficulties that brings.

In *Preaching to Strangers*, I criticized Will for sometimes reproducing in his sermons what Lindbeck described as the "experimental-expressive" account of religious conviction.[4] I noted, given the context of Duke Chapel in which you are basically preaching to strangers, it is very hard to avoid that strategy. However, I think Will's refusal to explain is a very effective mode of resistance to our endemic desire to make Jesus fit into our lives. To preach in that way risks "not being relevant to the real needs of people"; but the whole point of discipleship is to have our "real needs" transformed. Will's sermons, I believe, represent his attempt to remind us that no explanation is required because it is not "all about us."

Will's refusal to explain is the reason he also refuses to "translate" the gospel into other registers such as existentialism, moral lessons, or psychological insights. Words matter for Will. So, like the poet, he cannot try to explain the poem in words the poem does not use. Rather he must try to help us understand why it *has* to be in these words and not others. Of course, he has to use other words to help us understand why these words matter. But that is why preaching remains an art—an art that like all art is disciplined by imitating past and present masters.

That Will never explains helps explain why he is not afraid to be repetitious. In *With the Grain of the Universe*, I call attention to Barth's claim that "we can only repeat ourselves."[5] Barth could only repeat himself because he rightly understood that theology cannot be some position deeper than Scripture itself. Instead theology must be a witness to Scripture's witness to God's Word. So understood, theology is the attempt to assemble reminders that help us focus our attention on God.[6] The sermon is God's Word just to the extent that the proclaimed word does not replace the Word witnessed in Scripture.

Will, moreover, is a master of repetition. Some may get tired of him telling the story of Gladys,[7] but telling the story matters. Will has the impressive ability to tell the right story at the right time. His stories rarely illustrate a more basic, underlying point. Rather his stories *are* the point. Which means he must often tell the story without saying why he is telling the story. Either the story "works" or it does not. Will, therefore, must risk that his hearers will not "get" the story, but, then, that is why he has to tell it again. The Church calls the necessity to tell the story again and again preaching. Will never explains because he is a preacher.

Then Why Is Willimon So Popular?

If I am right about Willimon's refusal to explain, how do we account for his popularity? "Popularity" may be the wrong word, but at the very least some account needs to be given of why Will is in such demand as a preacher and lecturer. That he is one of the least obvious persons I know may account for why many find Will's preaching so compelling. That this good ol' boy from South Carolina has such interesting things to say is a mystery that attracts our interest. Of course, one of the reasons I suspect many find Will intriguing is that he does have something to say. In a world that is drowning in platitudes, hearing someone with something to say feels very much like discovering a wonderful land in the midst of a vast and uncharted ocean.

I often observe that Will is such a great preacher because he is an exemplary southern storyteller. Southern storytellers have never let the truth get in the way of telling a good story. Will is a collector of good stories that he makes more than they are by using one story to tell another story. To use one story to tell another story, of course, is a description of how the Bible works. The Bible is the story of the beginning and the end. In between is a string of stories that never end, except in another story. That is why preaching can never come to an end and why Will—who by disposition always wants to tell you another story—is such a great preacher.

Will is a great preacher because he helps us see the connections. When you cannot explain, you begin to realize that the work of preaching and theology is finding the connections between the stories. The Bible is an anthology of wildly different stories, and it is not immediately apparent how they interrelate. Preaching, and the theology that serves preaching, is the ongoing exploration of the Church to discover the connections. Christian doctrines are the hints that the Church has discovered that help us see the connections. The connections are made through the discoveries that the stories not only make possible but also demand.[8]

That Will always wants to tell you another story is, therefore, one reason he is in such high demand as a preacher. Theologically, he is committed to not being apologetic, which makes him a compelling Christian apologist. I think he is so because, as I have argued, he refuses to explain. By refusing to explain, he invites us into a world otherwise unimaginable, and we are fascinated and intrigued. We are fascinated and intrigued because the world called the gospel is at once so beautiful and so dangerous. We fear danger, but Will helps us see that without the beauty and danger of the gospel we are condemned to lives of boredom.

I should like to think, moreover, that one of the things Will and I share in common is neither of us can stand boredom. I hope our disdain for the boring is not because we need constant highs to sustain our lives. Actually we both live lives that I suspect most people would find boring. After all, we spend most of our time reading and writing—not exactly most people's idea of what it might mean to live an exciting life. What hopefully excites us, however, is that we find it extraordinary that God can make use of people as uninteresting as ourselves. God is great. Will never fails to remind us that God is great, and that is, I believe, one of the reasons so many find his preaching so compelling.

Yet who am I to explain the work of the Spirit?

CHAPTER 7

IT'S PECULIAR TO BE A PROPHET

William H. Willimon

This book is one of the best things that has happened to me. To be taken seriously by the fellow preachers for whom I have great respect—to be praised and criticized by them (we preachers generally don't care whether our preaching is extolled or condemned, as long as it is heard), to have them hear aspects of my preaching that I would never have noted myself, and to be the subject of their serious scrutiny—is wonderful.

The best thing that happened to me was to be called by God to preach. I've been a pastor to people whom God has called to care for the terribly poor, the awfully sick. I've known people whom God has called to suffer great deprivation and difficulty, or to be a witness to the gospel in dangerously hostile contexts. As for me, all I have to do is sit around and study Scripture, read books, eavesdrop on conversations between my people and God, compose sermons, and then stand up and speak to whoever will listen.

One of the worst things ever to happen to me was when I was summoned to Waco and declared one of the "Twelve Most Effective Preachers in the English-Speaking World." I got a gold medal and a three-volume history of Baylor University, but I also caught a lot of grief as well. For one thing, many of my fellow preachers despised me for being so designated, even though I had nothing to do with it. Envy is an ugly thing among the clergy. For another thing, being introduced as one of the "Twelve Most Effective Preachers" is a sure way to kill a sermon. No good sermon has been preached after that sort of introduction. It's like presenting a joke with, "I've got the funniest joke to tell you, the funniest thing you have ever heard."

It's never that funny.

But the worst thing about the award was that I was commended as "effective." I told my congregation that the folk at Baylor must not have checked out the moral state of my congregation when they declared me to be an "effective" preacher!

The trouble with "effective" is that it is not a judgment about the fidelity of a preacher or of a sermon, but rather an assessment of the results of the sermon in the congregation. Not, was the sermon biblical? Rather, did the sermon have consequences among the hearers? This is the view of preaching that Tom Long has called the most detrimental development in contemporary homiletics, what Tom calls "the turn to the listener." This turn has led to our current homiletical infatuation with rhetoric, communication strategies, and the techniques required for us to produce an "effective sermon." Anthropology replaces theology, and preaching slides into a way of talking that does not need God to make it work.

I am by no means immune from such anthropological concern. Hauerwas says that I really like to please, and he is right. In school, I was elected president of my class every year since the seventh grade. You don't get that way by being immune to public reaction. Despite my efforts to be otherwise, I really care what people think about my sermons. I really do value response, be it positive or negative. I can't stand not to be heard. When colleagues like Hauerwas, Rutledge, Dawn, Long, and Gomes, or former students like Turner and Malambri generally like what they hear, I love for them to tell me about it.

There is nothing inherently wrong in a preacher's wanting to be heard, wanting to be "effective," as we define effectiveness. In fact, be suspicious of any preacher who feigns disinterest in persuasion. A preacher who doesn't own and use carefully the power that is delivered into our hands through the speaking of the Word is dangerous.

What is wrong is to want to please one's hearers more than God, to measure the worth of the message by its effects. We pastors must, in our study, prayer, and spiritual practices, cultivate love, greater love for God even than for our people. We must see ourselves in service to the text rather than in subservience to the congregational context. I take Peter Gomes as my model in this. Peter somehow manages to show deep love and affection for his Harvard congregation mixed with contempt and condescension. I want to be like Peter. In preparation for writing *Pastor*, I surveyed the Church Fathers' writings on pastoral ministry. I was impressed by the sustained theme, so often articulated by the Fathers of the church when discussing the temptations faced by clergy, that clergy ought to cultivate a kind of contempt for the praise or the blame of their congregations. Pastors must love their people, but not in the wrong way. Preachers must be heard by our people, but on God's terms, not those of the people.

The temptation to pander to the people, to unduly love the *laos*, is virtually unavoidable for us preachers. We so want to be heard. An academic like Hauerwas can be content when he is read by his two dozen friends of the American Academy of Religion (though his writing suffers for it). But Jesus told us to shout from the housetops what the Holy Spirit had only whispered to us in our study (Matthew 10:27). In order to get them to hear the gospel, sometimes my lack of faith in the Third Person of the Trinity is unmasked. Since God isn't going to speak, I must. I strategize and sanitize the gospel. In leaning over to speak to my people, I fall in facedown among them, offering them a word little different from that which they could hear elsewhere—a superficial commentary on "the human condition," another technique for autosalvation, an inconsequential diatribe on the "important issues of our day," the psychological banalities of "Dr. Phil," the wisdom of "Dear Abby." Some Sundays, thanks to my desperate desire to be heard, the line between Duke Chapel and the Crystal Cathedral is perilously thin.

By God's grace on some (not all) Sundays, despite myself, I am "effective." People do hear the gospel and receive it. It is a gift, when it happens, not my achievement. I must be grateful, but not take too much credit for the hearing. To be honest, I have a better theology for Good Friday than Easter, despite Rutledge's praise for my Easter sermons. I've got a dozen reasons to explain why people do not hear a sermon, but only one reason for why they hear. Standing at the church door after service, their zombielike stares confirm all of my pessimism: Preaching is ineffective and outmoded, people are sinfully resistant to the gospel, I have not the gifts needed to communicate this sort of truth, I should have been more organized in my homiletical approach, yada, yada, yada—preaching is pointless.

But then someone surfaces, often the most clueless of sophomores, who has undeniably, irrefutably, quite obviously heard something, done business with the gospel, and been changed in the process, and my defeated, accommodated, pneumatically limp theology is challenged. Odd, how frightening it can be for a preacher actually to be heard. Frightening, to be used for such powerful purpose by God. Humbling, to see God take my poor homiletical thrashings and use them to take over the world. There is something quite reassuring, even comforting, in a preacher's belief in ineffectiveness. I say that I would like to be heard, but in reality, I don't mind when they don't hear. It confirms my skepticism about the New Testament's contention that preaching was an act of arson by the Holy Spirit. There is something oddly reassuring about Good Friday, but there is something deeply, dangerously challenging about Easter.

Barth says that we live between the time of Jesus' knocking and Jesus' entering.[1] A preacher thinks back, listening to the biblical text, those prior rappings at the door that have become Scripture. A preacher looks forward, to the present and future intrusions of the Word made flesh. All right, Dawn, I overuse "intrusion." Still, after thirty years of saying that I want God to speak to the Body of Christ through me, when God does, it still is disconcerting, intrusive—a surprise and a shock.

The predominant biblical reaction among Jesus' closest friends that first Easter was not joy but fear.

How I Preach

As I roam about the face of the earth, speaking with pastors about any number of subjects—weighty theological subjects upon which I am an expert five hundred miles outside Durham—no matter the subject, when time for discussion comes, there is always someone to ask, "How do you preach? Describe the process of your sermon preparation."

It is a fair question. The necessity of apprenticeship has been stressed in this book, as has the virtue of preaching as a collegial practice. I expect that I am not the most reliable person to say "how I preach" because I tend not to be all that self-reflective about my practice or to be completely honest about my homiletical limitations. Nevertheless, here are the steps I take on the way toward a sermon, or at least what I am willing to tell:

Get grabbed by a biblical text. I have various stratagems to accomplish this: prayer, study of the text, conversations with those who have given their lives to the study of Scripture (commentaries), and reading and listening to the sermons of others. I go to the text, in service to the congregation, hoping there to make a discovery, some news that is worth saying and that some struggling Christian is just dying to hear. One of my weaknesses is that I tend toward the weird in a biblical text. I fear that I am too fascinated by the incongruous, the strange, and the outrageous. I blame this tendency upon my long-term association with college students, but it could be due to my long friendship with Jesus. At best, this leads to some interesting sermons. At worst, I accentuate some tangential aspects of a text, highlight the unconventional and incongruous facets of Jesus at the expense of his more prosaic side. I read proverbs with less gusto than parables, and it shows in my preaching. Still, I do believe that the most interesting sermons arise out of a discovery that has been given to the preacher in the preacher's active conversation with the text.

Figure out how to break the news to the congregation. The challenge is to enable someone in the congregation to hear what I have heard. The way I see it, if the preacher discovers something to say, the preacher will find the means to say it. A message will summon its messenger. Calvin said that sermons must be twice born, once in the study and then again in the pulpit. That's what I want my sermons to be. As Barth put it, we preachers are like a person standing in the street, staring up at something in the sky, perhaps pointing in an upward direction. By such gestures, a crowd gathers, people stare up in that direction, straining to see what we see. All sermon design, form, illustration, and rhetorical strategy are gestures that we make before the congregation in service of proclamation. One of my weaknesses is that sometimes I get caught up in the art of a text, which leads to my preoccupation with the artfulness of the sermon. This sometimes engenders an unfortunate cleverness and a too self-conscious artistry that, in calling attention to itself, gets in the way of the gospel. Dawn's criticism of my sermons for being unorganized and therefore lacking some of the formative, transformative power that I claim to want them to have, is well-deserved criticism. My sermonic fits and starts, lack of transitions, and abrupt endings can make the sermon heard as more of an event, a rant, an ad hoc momentary encounter than a sustained, formative process for the listener. Guilty. Let me just say that, though Dawn says that she could only find a couple of my sermons to be well organized, at least I do a better job of organization than, say, the Gospel of Mark.

Tell them, as engagingly as I am able, what I have heard in the text. Rutledge, Gomes, and Dawn wish they had tapes of my sermons. I do not have the most polished delivery. I am self-conscious about the sound of my voice, my accent, my lack of eye contact, and my rather wooden gesturing. Delivery is that aspect of preaching that is least taught, least valued in seminary homiletics courses, but most prized among congregations. Delivery, presentation, voice, and eye control—the bodily, visual, performative aspects of preaching—have become increasingly important to me over the years, though sometimes you could not tell by listening to me preach. Most African American preachers have not forgotten that preaching is an oral event, something that is seen and heard, not something that is read.

Quit just in time for God to get hold of them. In this book I have been praised, or critiqued, for my infamous abrupt sermon endings. Partly my hasty retreat from a sermon is due to my simply not knowing how to stop. Also, I have always been told, since the days of my youth, that I talk too much. I don't trust silence. So I try to discipline myself, at least in my preaching, not to go on, not to say more than I know, not to reiterate more than I ought. I would like to think that I have been influenced by Jesus' rhetorical strategies. He refused to provide a conclusion to many of his best parables. Over the years I have learned the importance of getting out of God's way, of attempting to be as transparent as possible so that some of the divine light might shine through, of creating some space, a gap, that leaves God room to roam among the listeners. It appears, from my experience, that the Holy Spirit loves to slide into that area between the text and the congregation. As Long says, discipleship is the point, and the test of a sermon is embodiment and performance by the congregation. Therefore the preacher needs to end leaving something unsaid, unexplained, unfinished, some room similar to that created by Mark's Gospel or the ending of Luke's Acts. I heard Henri Nouwen say that we pastors ought to take care in how we leave a hospital room, the last thing that we say being the most important, an invitation for our pastoral conversations to become encounters with God. Some of my best sermons are not in this book because they began when my "sermon" ended, when the congregation took over the sermon and finished what I could not. The sermon really began when they enacted, embodied the gospel in the world, the gospel that I could only point toward in my sermon in church.

Am I a Prophet?

It is more than a little embarrassing for this book to call me a "prophet." I don't believe that my preaching deserves such an exalted designation. I am much too "effective" to be called a prophet. Besides, the terms "prophet" and "prophetic preaching" are so conflicted and misunderstood that I would never apply them to myself or my work in the pulpit. Only God can call a preacher a "prophet."

What I know about the word *prophet*, I have learned from Walter Brueggemann. He says that "a prophet, in the biblical tradition, is someone with uncommon access to matters of God's will and purpose that usually remain hidden to other people."[2] Prophets crop up from time to time in Yahweh's history with Israel, often during times of national crisis, such as the eighth century. Yet their words are daringly out of sync with what the community may long to hear in its crisis. Prophetic preaching worries more about listening to and speaking for God and less about listener approval, visible results, church growth, seeker sensitivity, user friendliness, and other ways that we pay more attention to what the congregation is able to hear rather than what the Trinity is able to say. And as I've admitted, I like to be liked, I hanker to be heard, and I am eager to be "effective." Too many preachers pay for my *Pulpit Resource* or buy my books for me to be a "prophet." I preached to twelve hundred people last Sunday, a fairly average service at Duke Chapel. I doubt that Amos could have mustered a dozen.

As Hauerwas says, I come from the South, which explains a lot about me. Amos was also a Southerner. But prophets are not explained by reference to the circumstances of their birth. Prophets appear from out of nowhere, with inadequate precedents and neither portfolio, nor preparation, nor anything in their background that explains anything about their preaching: Amos, the farmer from the South; Jeremiah, the youth. This is a biblical way of stressing that a prophet's authorization rests on the miracle of divine vocation, not on the prophet's faith development. That vocation enables the prophet to utter the characteristic, "Thus saith the Lord." Prophetic preaching is unashamedly "miraculous"—it rests upon divine summons and is a gift, grace, an act of God, not an achievement of the preacher. The prophet's call means that the prophet's words arise neither from royal patronage nor popular appeal. A prophet's message is miraculous, that is, an act of God. Most of my sermons are too self-consciously created by me, are too intruded upon by the limitations or expectations of the listeners, to be called "prophetic." "Predictable" (rather than "miraculous") is the word that comes to mind after hearing too many of my sermons.

Prophets tend to read history liturgically, a matter of conflicted worship. Our morality is derivative of the sort of God we think we've got. Therefore prophets keep talking about God, keep rendering God as the proper subject of their preaching. God's speech is their obsession. The community's false faith in money, power, and armaments is characterized as a failure to worship the true and living God, as idolatry. Atheism, our modern obsession, is uninteresting to the prophets. In their minds, everything— politics, sex, marriage, children, military hardware, the poor—is at heart a question of, "Which God do you worship?" I came to Duke first to teach courses in liturgics. Sunday, sometime between eleven and noon, is my most intense experience of my vocation as a preacher, a weekly reminder of who I am and why I am here. If church is not about God, it is pointless. If ministry is not about the constant construal of all life under God, then ministry is mere misery. If I am "prophetic" at all, it is in my continuing obsession with God, my sustained excitement over how odd a God we've got, my unceasing delight over the queer way that our God talks.

Come to think of it, perhaps I'm suitably called a prophet because prophets work primarily through words. When all is said and done by government press releases, snips of insight on the evening news, the cute presentations of *USA Today*, or the pompous self-assertions of the *New York Times*, as Brueggemann (citing Walt Whitman) says, finally comes the prophet to tell a truth that's too large to be uttered in anything less than poetry. The prophet is a poet, not the carping social critic of some contemporary characterizations. Prophetic preaching tends toward metaphor and highly charged symbolic discourse. Through words, imaginative metaphors, and figurative gestures a prophet invites the covenant community to a reconstrual of reality, *sub specie aeternatis*. I love words, love working with a loquacious God who refuses to abandon the conversation, love nothing better than to have reality brought to speech. My mother said that when I was four I begged her to read *Winnie-the-Pooh* fifteen times in succession, even though I could not have understood anything in the book. After that she knew that, whatever I did in life, it would have to be done with words.

As Hauerwas notes, I've got this irrational regard for the Church. My inability to escape the Church embodies Hauerwas's communitarian theology better than he does. I do not approve of the behavior of the Church or the way she makes her money, but even though she can be a whore, she is my mother. So although I try not to be overly influenced by my hearers and their regard for my "effectiveness," I say what I say in service to the Church. My peculiar service is to nurture, to evoke, and to nourish love for a very interesting God. Long's chapter on my preaching and discipleship gets to the heart of what I think I'm doing. The test of my preaching is, finally, not the high regard of masters of the art like those who appear in this book, but rather the shape of my congregation. If God has not used me to call forth a people who, at least in their better moments, here and there, are the visible Body of Christ, then my preaching has no point and homiletical disorganization is the least of my worries. The purpose of prophetic preaching is the production of a community of prophets called the Body of Christ. The preacher is not the surrogate prophet for the congregation, but rather the one who gives the people the words, the images, and the demonstration of dependency upon God that equips them for the prophetic ministry that is theirs by virtue of their baptism. Each week I must lay the story that is the gospel on them, must keep pointing them toward Jesus, must stoke, fund, and fuel their gospel-induced imaginations. By these words I have faith, even after three decades of doing it, that they have a good chance of hearing that God really does intend to get back what belongs to God and that they are God's main means of accomplishing God's will for the world.

And guess who gets to tell them that's true?

CHAPTER 8

SAYING IT, FOR GOD'S SAKE

William F. Malambri III

So what? What is the point of all this Willimon chatter? Who is he to engender such a discourse and why do we even care? Why should we even keep this book in the ever-deepening volumes of our study's bookshelf, especially if what these authors have said is true, namely that no book will enable us to preach exactly like Will, nor should we want to?

But we do want to, don't we? We want to influence thousands (even hundreds would be nice) with our salient words and pithy stories. We want to convey the common in such a way that the congregation is moved by the uncommon, the astounding grace of God, which comes with powerful claims on our lives. We want to have insights into the Word of God that captivate and inspire. We want these things because, like anyone who seeks to do his or her best, we want "success." Ironically, that's the last thing Will wants for us.

Ironically, someone who has achieved the status of *the Reverend Dr. Dean* William H. Willimon is opposed to success, at least "success" as the world defines it. "Success," in the eyes of the world, is based on numbers served (see McDonald's) or immediate effect (see caffeine). What Will wants for us is faithfulness, which is rarely as efficient as corporations or as instantaneous as substances. Faithfulness is participating in God's dramatic, albeit sometimes imperceptibly slow, ways of drawing persons closer to the God revealed in Christ and deeper into discipleship. So while Will looks "successful" before the world, his prayer is that he be "faithful" before God. Such is our prayer—to be faithful in our living and proclaiming the Christian faith.

The question, then, is not as much "so what," as "so how." How can we be the faithful preachers God calls us to be? The answer lies in our willingness to proclaim the Truth as we know it to a world who knows other truths and to Christians who seem to prefer them. When we, for the sake of the gospel of Jesus Christ, deny ourselves, take up our crosses, and follow Christ, we are faithful—as painful as that faithfulness may be. When we, for the sake of the gospel, state the gospel truth, we are following Christ, regardless of who (and how many) is willing to remain to be challenged, provoked, and healed by him.

So, then, how are we to preach?

Say It

Preaching is a great gift and challenge. The vast majority of those who preach are pastors, persons whose vocation involves more than rhetorical exhibition. Most people who preach are unable to avoid their audience's reaction because their audience is the congregation, the people with whom they serve God not only on Sundays, but also throughout the week. Thankfully, most pastors cannot avoid their audience, nor do they want to. They recognize that their task is not to work the congregation into a lather or condemn them for their sinfulness, but to proclaim the gospel faithfully and then, side by side with the laborers in the field, seek to live the gospel daily. It is this daily laboring that births a love between congregations and pastors.

Pastors know something of the hardships of congregation members. They have seen them struggle with the faith or with living righteously or with the conflicting, confusing world that their faith must enter each day. Pastors know from their own frailties and from the people they have stood alongside that being a Christian is not easy, nor formulaic. Being a Christian is hard and contextual.

Knowing the suffering of congregants, pastors are understandably wary of overt exhortation. Knowing the prevailing cultural mind-set of "me and mine" before "you or anyone else's," pastors are understandably wary of compassionate coaxing. We are caught between our own compassion for others, earnest self-appraisal of our own weaknesses, and great concern for the declining dedication to discipleship.

We wanted to know how to preach in this climate. What is it about Will Willimon's sermons that we can be castigated and encouraged, inspired and challenged, comforted and discomforted all at the same time? So we asked him, seeking but one straightforward suggestion. Instead, we got Willimon at his parabolic best:

> You may know that my father-in-law, Mr. Parker, was a minister. During the time my wife and I were dating he was a District Superintendent and detested that he was relegated to the pews, rather than the pulpit, on most Sundays. One Sunday, while I was still considering seminary, the Parker family took me to church with them. That particular Sunday, the preacher was a master of ambiguity and equivocation. Mr. Parker squirmed in his pew as the preacher carefully qualified just about every statement made in the sermon. Mr. Parker withdrew his large railroad watch from his pocket at five-minute intervals throughout the sermon, the watch that had been given to him by some thankful congregation of the past. He would gaze at his watch, shake his head, thrust it back into his pocket, and groan slightly. The poor preacher continued to flail away, thrashing at his subject rather than delivering it.
>
> "We need to be more committed to Christ . . . but not to the point of fanaticism, not to the point of neglect of our other important responsibilities."
>
> "We need to have a greater dedication to the work of the church. Now I don't mean that the church is the only significant organization of which you are a member. Most of us have obligations to various community groups."

And on, and on. Every five minutes, with some ceremony, Mr. Parker withdrew his gold railroad watch from his pocket, opened it, looked at it, remained surprised that so little time had been used, closed it, and slapped it back in his pocket with regret.

After the service, all of us in the District Superintendent's party brushed right past Mr. Milk Toast with barely a word of greeting. Mr. Parker led us down the sidewalk back to the District parsonage, like ducks in a row. He went right through the front door and charged up the stairs. Pausing midway, he whirled around, shaking a finger at me and thundering, "Young man, if God should be calling you into the pastoral ministry, and if you should ever be given a church by the bishop, and if God ever gives you a word to say, *for God's sake would you say it!*"

Willimon concluded that this is the only lesson in homiletics that Mr. Parker ever gave him and that "it was enough." What he didn't say, because he didn't need to, was "go and do likewise." Like the Rabbi he follows, Willimon answered with a story and we knew our task—to say it.

It's your task, too. We, as homeleticians, have a responsibility to say it. The specifics of what "it" is may change each time we enter the pulpit, but the responsibility never wanes. It is not our task to apologize for the Scripture, to relativize it until it meets our worldview, or to psychologize it for the sake of modern sensibilities. It is also not our task to use Scripture as a weapon or as a means to further our personal agenda. Scripture is not our tool, we are Scripture's tool.

We are the mouthpieces for the texts that birth our preaching. We are the spokespersons for the Spirit who inspires our words. But we are not the author of holy writ or the defender of Christ's integrity. Think what you will of the Gospels' miracles, but preach them that others may know their truth. Think what you will of Paul's pious pronouncements, but preach them that others may be moved to holiness. Think what you will of Scriptures' continuous praise of Almighty God, but preach praise that others may give God the glory.

Mr. Parker imparted on Will Willimon the burden of saying the truth as clearly and unapologetically as he can. Willimon gives us the same task. We are to let the Word of God reign supreme, qualifying and critiquing popular psychology, cultural trends, and other external influences that distract from our clearest source of God's revelation since God's own Son.

Granted, there are times when this source is "clear as mud." There are times when we are honest enough to admit that we do not know what Jesus or Isaiah or Paul meant. There are times when we do have an idea of what they meant and do not like it. But our ignorance or our dislike of the Scriptures does not excuse our insurrection. We are to stand beneath the cross and behind the Bible, saying to the best of our ability what God has given us to say. We are to give to those who hear our fearful and trembling voices the gift of God's Word, not our distilled version of it. For however smart, sophisticated, and savvy we may be, our words pale in the presence of the Word.

Say It Well

Rick Lischer, professor of preaching, describes the sermon as crossing a stream. We have to leave one bank and cross to the other, but the rocks we walk across might not be in a straight line. They, more likely, will move us down a circuitous route, all the while leading us toward the final destination. Preaching, like crossing the stream, is directional, but not linear. Lischer cites Will Willimon as an example of this type of preaching.

Indeed, Will is not linear, as lauded in this volume by Stanley Hauerwas and questioned by Marva Dawn. There is often a circular flow to his sermons, a kind of rapid presentation of images that can confound and illuminate simultaneously (just like the Scriptures they reflect). But he never begins the journey across the stream without knowing which rocks he will use and where he wants to land on the other bank. Traversing with Will through a sermon may put the hearers' tranquillity at risk, but, if they are willing to go with him, they will land on the other side and be the better for it, even if they had to roll up their pants legs at times to get there.

His loose, sometimes dangerous, often entertaining, always intriguing style is not without labor, nor is it accidental. It is the result of crafting, of taking the time to prepare. One of the first "steps" Will takes in the long journey of preparing a sermon is to read a text both prayerfully and playfully. He reads the text seeking God's direction, always with an eye to the strange. Will is drawn to the oddities of Scripture passages. He likes to find the parts of the text that just do not fit our worldview—and then he exploits them.

Those oddities often capture us because they bring life to texts that have been talked to death. They serve to pique our interest, draw us in, cause us to let our guard down, and seduce us, only to be blindsided by a convicting word that challenges our lifestyle or the prevailing influences with which the faith must battle.

And battle the faith we must, Willimon's sermons demonstrate. Our faith is not some amalgamation of whatever makes us "happy" (whatever that might mean), but it is a higher calling to the true joy of discipleship. This means, among other things, following the call to discipleship to the exclusion of the competing temptations jockeying for our commitments. Or, as the bumper-sticker slogan states, "to be in the world, not of the world."

For all his "alien" status, Willimon is quite in the world. Part of his crafting a sermon is his restless wresting of the surrounding culture. When Will made a reference in preaching class to *Eyes Wide Shut*, I was forced to admit, "I was not allowed to watch that movie." Will's taste in movies aside, it is his insatiable appetite for his surroundings that makes his "alien" status so intriguing. He reads incessantly and is formed by the Patristics and contemporaries such as Karl Barth, Stanley Hauerwas, and Walter Brueggemann. But his formation is not exclusive to those books relegated to the "religion section." Flannery O'Connor is a primary influence on Willimon, and he continually engages the surrounding culture through periodicals, movies, and even by listening to comedians. "Listen to anyone who tells a story well," he advises, "and they [comedians] tell the best ones."

How can someone who engages and absorbs so much of the prevailing culture be so critical of it? Will can be critical *precisely because* of his absorption. When Willimon critiques the culture that is invading the Church's pews, it is not from a pious television studio in Virginia or Texas, it is with a depth of understanding at how the world comes at us, and with knowledge of what seems so likable about it. Therefore, his illustration from a movie that has fascinated his audience does not come from a condemnatory, bullying pulpit, but with an understanding of why the movie spoke to us and what its speaking to us says about us.

Willimon knows his hearers because he is not afraid to know himself. He knows what tempts us, what clamors for our devotion, and what we are willing to serve as idols. Will knows because he lives in our world. He also knows how to speak to it because he wants his hearers to recall their allegiance beyond this world. Will knows that if he is to be saved, it is God who will save him and to that God he is committed. To move his hearers in their allegiance to this God, he crafts, with great skill, powerful sermons that use this world and plunder this world, only to transcend this world.

All in all, Will's sermons say it well because they are well prepared. He begins early (often three or more months out), praying over and exegeting the text. This allows him time to listen to the world, to his hearers, and, of course, to the text, as he considers what it is that God would have him proclaim. He is constantly mining for the right word to move his hearers to new depths of praise, discipleship, and understanding. With this ample lead time and committed ear, Will's sermons can germinate into the right word for the right time, said well and said appropriately.

Say It Appropriately

Homiletics classes provide a curious environment for teaching preaching. They often require studious exegetical work, delivery of sermons in a most atypical environment (rarely is one feeling "worshipful" when the professor calls your name to deliver a sermon to pencil-clad peers), and immediate reflection and

responses from peers and professors. The skills gained from gird-
ing up one's loins and standing before this awkward setting are
useful and appreciated when one must stand before congregants
eager to hear the message.

Studying homiletics under Will Willimon, I found one consistent mantra: Preach the text you have as the text is given.
"Reflect the mood and genre of the text in your style and content," we were told. So much emphasis was placed on our reflecting the text that I began to wonder, "Why not simply read the
text several times, let it wash over the congregation, and let the
Scriptures speak for themselves?" My question was logical, for I
knew my feeble attempts at interpretation would only detract
from Scripture anyway.

It turns out my feebleness was to be used. There is something
to interpreting the Scriptures for the context in which one finds
oneself. As absolutely critical as unrolling the scroll and reading
it before our sisters and brothers is, there is also something crucial in shaping words, shaped by the Word, to help shape we who
live under the Word. Pastors are called to preach from beneath
the cross and behind the Bible, but not to breach the gift of
proclamation born within us. We have been gifted by the Spirit
to open the Word of God before others, and to deny that is no
less than leaving our cross for another to bear.

Part of the Spirit's gift for our preaching is the gift of preparation. Unlike the unwilling or lazy preachers who claim superiority for their "openness to the Spirit's leading," Willimon reminds
us that the Spirit's leading begins many months before the day of
proclamation. That is not to say that the Spirit does not work the
morning of; Willimon readily admits some of his most important
editing is at 8:30 A.M. on the Sunday the sermon is to be delivered. The point is that the Spirit has been at work on that sermon, in that preacher, and in those who are to hear the
proclaimed Word, for some time. As Willimon likes to note, "if
the first time you pray, 'May the words of my mouth and the meditations of all our hearts be acceptable in your sight, O Lord' is
ten seconds before you start preaching, then you have not given
God much time to put the words in your mouths and to prepare
your hearts."

Preaching is a craft that requires the work of preparation, including the work of knowing to whom we preach. Context does not dictate content, but it does determine details. Will's wife Patsy noted that his sermons were much more academic in the churches before coming to the academy. Once at Duke he became more emotional in presentation and content. Will has chosen to be context appropriate. It is not that the content is all that different; he preaches Christ crucified in the farm church and Duke Chapel (built on farm funds), but he fills out the details based on his hearers. He knows the academicians have read scholarship, but have they allowed Jesus to be their Lord above research, peer review, or self-adulation? He knows the farmer has placed a great deal of trust in God's sovereignty and showers of blessings, but has that farmer considered how Mark's presentation differs from Matthew's and why?

Context is important; it is our way of knowing what to say and how. We must ask ourselves, "Who are these hearers?" We must consider their station in life, their experiences with God, their Christian maturity, and their customs. Willimon once pointed out that some churches need to have their complacency challenged and need to be cajoled into justice ministry. Other churches, we were surprised to hear from Will, relish being cajoled and might need to hear more about grace and our inability to earn it. Their customs, their histories, help determine how we shape the unchanging message.

Thus, to preach well we need to know the congregation's customs and their stories. We need to invest the time required to hear from the members—who they are and from whence they come. We need to exhibit our unflappable presence in the good times and the bad, demonstrating that whether or not they like what we say, we will still be there to say it. They need to see us in the hospital and the cemetery before they will be ready to hear us say hard truths from the pulpit.

Once we know them, then we can speak with new depth and power. Once they trust us, then they can hear with greater openness and a willing suspension of distrust. Our preaching will then become even more appropriate to our context, and the Word of God will become all the more exacting.

Say It Often

I enjoy bicycling. During a group ride, while reflecting on preaching, I noted the effectiveness of a simple cycling expression, "car back." Even when the paceline of riders is fifteen cyclists long, the message that a car is about to pass the entire group can be disseminated from the last cyclist to the front rider before the car is able to pass them. Sometimes, for the sake of time or to preserve precious breath, the expression will be reduced to "back," but with no less effectiveness, as the riders are conditioned to keep toward the shoulder of the road whenever a staccato "-ack" is uttered from behind. The cyclists know what they are listening for, and they respond to it.

Preachers once had a similar luxury. They once were confident that the congregants knew what to listen for and would respond accordingly. A simple reference to a biblical character was sufficient to recall that story and its meaning. A slight nod toward Jesus' ethics, and the congregation was on board with wherever the preacher was going. We no longer can expect this of our hearers; we cannot count on their knowing what they are listening for.

So we must preach with repetition. We must be willing to go back to the Word and its call on us because the hearers may not have gotten it the first (or seventh) time. I think this is why Will's story of the outraged student leaving the Chapel is not overdone. It is done, but not overdone. As a critical listener/reader, I cannot believe that there have been as many brazen students calling into question Willimon's offensive stories (which, he happily reports to them, are *Jesus'* stories). "Where did you get that story?" they are said to ask; "it offends me," we're told they say. To which Will tells the offended students that he envies their fresh hearing (read: ignorance) of the Scripture, that they, more than those who have heard that story all of their lives, got what Jesus intended.

I hope (and expect) that Will has faced such a student before. I hope this has occurred on multiple occasions. I doubt that it has happened as many times as he has told it, and I know that it has not happened to as many preachers as have used it. The illustration has been done, but not overdone. While we have no real notion of how many times someone has been brazen enough to ask Will where he gets that stuff, we do know it is less than how many times that stuff has proved odd and difficult. We know that whether or not the offended party admitted it, she or he should have been offended—offended because his or her (our) lifestyle often offends the gospel; offended because the stories Jesus tells and the implications of Jesus' stories are shocking, even for those who have heard them rehearsed time and again.

Psychologists or old wives or both have told us that it takes seven times for someone to learn something. Willimon's sermons indicate that he has not followed this tale. Rather, he gets his guidance from Jesus, who tells us it takes seventy times seven times for disciples to learn something. Forgiveness, like other practices of discipleship, is a hard practice to acquire. A single sermon admonishing the congregation to forgive one another will not suffice. In training disciples of a crucified Lord who cries from the cross, "Father, forgive them," repetitive rehearsal is required.

And yet, while repetitive, Will's sermons are not redundant. He is able to find multiple ways to make his point. The material remains fresh, even if it is sometimes leftovers. Such is the power of the gospel. Preachers do not have to look to books of virtues or self-help drivel to find fresh approaches to "speaking to" their hearers. We simply have to discipline ourselves to spend time in God's Word and let the Word wash over us in new and exciting ways. In the process, drawing from a well that has been tapped for centuries, we will give living water to a thirsting congregation.

Say It, for God's Sake

I went to Wofford College with Will's children. They provided an entirely different vantage point from which to understand our illustrious mentor. While discussing this book project with Will's son, William, he told us that he wanted his father to go ahead and write the great American novel. He knows that Will has spent enough time with Flannery O'Connor, William Faulkner, and Lee Smith to bring his southern storytelling to a new height. He also knows that there is a broader audience and, therefore, bigger dividends for such work. But, alas, he also knows best that his father does not write sermons or books for financial reward. His father writes and preaches for God's sake.

William's grandfather, Will's father-in-law, exclaimed, "For God's sake, say it." This is Willimon's gift and our task. What he says, he says for God's sake. His critique of The United Methodist Church, which has not won many friends, is because he wants his denomination to follow Christ, for God's sake. His challenge of the powers that be, those in Christendom and those in the political and social structures, has not been gladly received, but it has been an important witness to the gospel's challenge to those powers.

What we learn in Will's preaching and writing, he learns through spiritual disciplines. He learns in his prayer life and in his devotional reading that we are not yet where God would have us be. He also learns that our great efforts will not get us there. Our efforts are the appropriate responses to God's grace, but without God's grace, they are as forward-moving as a treadmill.

The great insight Will's preaching gives us is that failure is not to be feared, but to be expected. We are preaching about and empowered by the God who chose the cross. That, in the eyes of the world, is absolute failure. But to those who are being saved, it is the power of God. When we assume the mantle of the pulpit, we stand beneath the cross that looks like failure and, our voices joined with Will Willimon's and the great cloud of witnesses', proclaim the hard and gracious truth of the cross, the truth we hear in the Scriptures. When we preach, we say it for God's sake.

Notes

1. Why Willimon?

1. "Desiring too desperately to communicate at any cost can lead us into apostasy. The odd way in which God has saved us presents a never-ending challenge to those who are called to talk about it." William H. Willimon, *The Intrusive Word: Preaching to the Unbaptized* (Grand Rapids: William B. Eerdmans, 1994), 18.

2. Neil Postman, *Amusing Ourselves to Death: Public Discourse in the Age of Show Business* (New York: Penguin Books, 1985). Another point that Postman makes about our media culture and the "TV age" is that it forms people who can absorb massive amounts of information without ever being truly affected by it. Using the methods of the entertainment culture within or in place of the sermon reinforces the notion that one can experience the gospel without doing much in response, without transformation as a result. This is one of my concerns about Mel Gibson's box office hit *The Passion of the Christ*.

3. Or, as Will Willimon puts it in a recent article, "Once you've heard those rhythms and syncopations for the millionth time in TV ads, it is very difficult to wrest them from the grip of consumerism, almost impossible for them not to transform Jesus into just another means of stroking my narcissistic ego." "It's Hard to be Seeker-Sensitive When You Work for Jesus" in *Circuit Rider* 27, no. 5 (September-October 2003).

4. Or, as Eugene Peterson puts it, the culture of consumerism and entertainment threatens to trivialize the Church's witness: "In a religious culture that relentlessly commercializes every aspect of the church's life, auctioning its preachers to the highest bidder and marketing its crosses, it is increasingly difficult to take any of it seriously. When advertising and entertainment provide the dominant modes of discourse for Christian worship and its preaching and teaching, accommodation to the culture takes precedence over sacrifice for truth. For millions of people, silliness is far more in evidence than sanctity."

Under the Unpredictable Plant: An Exploration in Vocational Holiness (Grand Rapids: William B. Eerdmans, 1992), 146.

5. Willimon has pointed out, "The irony is that any book on self-help is a lie. If our help were exclusively in ourselves, then why the heck must we pay $19.95 plus postage for somebody else's book in order to help ourselves?" "New World, New You," unpublished sermon, March 25, 2001.

6. Or, as Willimon puts it, "A comfortably domesticated church tends to abandon its theological language and replace it with the language of secular therapy, for that is the mode of salvation currently affirmed by the dominant culture—the goal of self-fulfillment." *Pastor: The Theology and Practice of Ordained Ministry* (Nashville: Abingdon, 2002), 94-95.

7. No faithful sermon is completely "original" because it is derived from the biblical text in conversation with the Christian tradition. However, taking another's work wholesale and passing it off as one's own is theft.

8. Study is not high on the priority list of many pastors these days. Instead, many clergypersons fall victim to models of ministry that require them to rush around at a breathless pace, attending to the felt needs of their parishioners. For a discussion of these different models, including a critique of contemporary images of ministry, see *Pastor: The Theology and Practice of Ordained Ministry*, 55-74. See also Willimon's account of this dilemma in *Character and Calling: Virtues of the Ordained Life* (Nashville: Abingdon, 2000), 15-31.

9. Marva J. Dawn, *A Royal "Waste" of Time: The Splendor of Worshiping God and Being Church for the World* (Grand Rapids: William B. Eerdmans, 1999).

10. "Good preaching requires so wide a range of gifts and skills. It is no wonder that some have asked if it can be taught at all. 'Preachers are born not made.' Although the natural gifts of the preacher count for much, good preaching is an art, not magic. It must be learned. As with any art, preaching is an alloy of gifts and training, natural inclination, and cultivated dispositions. Because preaching is an art, the best methods of homiletical education tend to be modes of apprenticeship—a novice looking over the shoulder of an experienced master of the art in order to get the insights, moves, and gestures required to practice that art." Willimon, *Pastor: The Theology and Practice of Ordained Ministry*, 153. Cf. the introduction to *Pastor: A Reader for Ordained Ministry* (Nashville: Abingdon, 2002).

11. Richard Lischer, *The Preacher King: Martin Luther King Jr. and the Word that Moved America* (Oxford: Oxford University Press, 1995), 69-70. Lischer's entire chapter "Apprenticed to the Word" discusses King's formation in homiletics. Cf. Willimon's discussion of imitation in *Pastor: The Theology and Practice of Ordained Ministry*, 156-57. Willimon points out that "John Wesley told his preachers to preach all of his sermons before they attempted to preach their own." Clearly, Mr. Wesley understood the importance of apprenticeship and imitation.

12. The origin of this statement is debated. However, one likely possibility is Dan Maultsby, Dean of Wofford College, Spartanburg, S.C. Noted theologian, as well as colleague and friend of Willimon, Stanley Hauerwas has been known to respond to this statement by saying, "True, and most of them are mine!"

13. He has published in excess of sixty-seven volumes—even he has lost count at this point!

14. *Word, Water, Wine and Bread: How Worship Has Changed Over the Years* (Valley Forge, Pa.: Judson Press, 1980); *Preaching and Leading Worship* (Louisville: Westminster / John Knox Press, 1984); *Sunday Dinner* (Nashville: Upper Room Books, 1983); *Remember Who You Are: Baptism and the Christian Life* (Nashville: Upper Room Books, 1988); *With Glad and Generous Hearts: A Personal Look at Sunday Worship* (Nashville: Upper Room Books, 1986); *Liturgy and Learning through the Life Cycle*, with John H. Westerhoff III (Akron: OSL Publications, 1980, 1994).

15. *Lord of the Congaree* (Orangeburg, S.C.: Sandlapper Press, 1972).

16. *Reading with Deeper Eyes: The Love of Literature and the Life of Faith* (Nashville: Upper Room Books, 1998).

17. *Rekindling the Flame: Strategies for a Vital United Methodism*, with Robert Wilson (Nashville: Abingdon, 1987), and *A New Connection: Reforming The United Methodist Church* (Nashville: Abingdon, 1995).

18. *The Abandoned Generation: Rethinking Higher Education* (Grand Rapids: William B. Eerdmans, 1995).

19. *Downsizing the U.S.A.*, with Thomas Naylor (Grand Rapids: William B. Eerdmans, 1997).

20. *Good Bye High School, Hello College* (Nashville: Dimensions for Living, 1993), and *On Your Own But Not Alone: Life After College* (Nashville: Dimensions for Living, 1995).

21. Some of his other major works not cited elsewhere in this chapter are: *Resident Aliens: Life in the Christian Colony*, with Stanley Hauerwas (Nashville: Abingdon, 1989); *Where Resident Aliens Live: Exercise for Christian Practice*, with Stanley Hauerwas (Nashville: Abingdon, 1996); *Lord, Teach Us to Pray: The Lord's Prayer and the Christian Life*, with Stanley Hauerwas (Nashville: Abingdon, 1996); *The Truth About God: The Ten Commandments in Christian Life*, with Stanley Hauerwas (Nashville: Abingdon, 1999); *Worship as Pastoral Care* (Nashville: Abingdon, 1979); and *Acts: Interpretation: A Bible Commentary for Teaching and Preaching* (Louisville: Westminster / John Knox Press, 1988). In addition, he has written a total of five hundred weeks of *Pulpit Resource*, a lectionary-based homiletical tool.

22. His magnum opus, *Pastor: The Theology and Practice of Ordained Ministry*, includes 474 footnotes that cite over 271 commentators on ministry, including hundreds of citations from Patristic and Reformation sources. This demonstrates Willimon's conviction that the way forward in the pastoral ministry is based on a continuing conversation with those who have preceded us in this craft.

23. *Christian Century* 120, no. 17 (August 23, 2003): 31-33.

24. Ibid., 141-70.

25. Ibid., 144.

26. The post-Enlightenment assumption in the West is that "rationality" can be universally defined. Drawing heavily on the work of Alasdair MacIntyre, Willimon contends that even our notions of rationality are traditioned—formed by a particular narrative of existence. In other words, what constitutes being "rational" is already the result of a conversion, though in Western culture we are scarcely aware of it. What Christianity requires, according to Willimon, is a different conversion—a transformation wrought through the Holy Spirit. MacIntyre's most pertinent work to this discussion is *Whose Justice? Which Rationality?* (Notre Dame: University of Notre Dame Press, 1988).

27. Therefore he doggedly refuses to make the Church's language subservient to the world's way of speaking. "The modern church has been willing to use everyone's language but its own. . . . Unable to preach Christ and him crucified, we preach humanity and it improved. As Walter Brueggemann said, when the preacher is uncertain about speech, a great deal of energy is expended reassuring the listener that nothing will be said that would require *conversion* in order to be understood, certainly nothing that would be regarded by cultural despisers as either foolish or weak" (emphasis added). *Peculiar Speech: Preaching to the Baptized* (Grand Rapids: William B. Eerdmans, 1992), 9. Elsewhere he writes, "We preachers so want to be heard that we are willing to make the gospel more accessible than it really is, to remove the scandal, the offense of the cross, to deceive people into thinking that it is possible to hear without *conversion*" (emphasis added). *Intrusive Word*, 19. And, in another tirade on the subject, "In leaning over to speak to the world, I fear that we may have fallen in! When, in our sermons, we sought to use sermons to build a bridge from the old world of the Bible to the new modern world, the traffic was only moving in one direction on that interpretive bridge. . . . It was always the modern world telling the Bible what's what. . . . The Bible doesn't want to speak to the modern world. The Bible wants to change, convert the modern world." "The Five-Minute Preaching Workshop," in *Pulpit Resource* 31, no. 2 (Inner Grove Heights, Minn.: Logos Productions, 2003).

28. Cardinal Suhard was the archbishop of Paris through the difficult times of the German occupation of France during World War II.

29. Dorothy Day, *Selected Writings: By Little and By Little*, ed. Robert Ellsberg (New York: Orbis Books, 1998), xv.

30. *The Intrusive Word*, 22.

31. One caveat is in order at this point. Imitating a master craftsperson will, no doubt, hone the skills of a growing preacher and help him or her discover and use his or her own gifts. While no preacher should try to become another, studying different masters will help one to, in the words of Zan Holmes, "realize one's preaching potential."

32. Willimon, "Our Failure, God's Success," unpublished sermon, April 22, 2001.

33. Cf. *Pastor: The Theology and Practice of Ordained Ministry*, 155.

34. See *Intrusive Word*, 18, 24. Cf. *Pastor: The Theology and Practice of Ordained Ministry*, 144.

35. This is a theme in much of Yoder's work. More specifically, see *The Politics of Jesus: Vicit Agnus Noster* (Grand Rapids: William B. Eerdmans, 1972, second edition 1994). While the work as a whole deals with this theme, see pp. 234-37, in particular, for a critique of "effectiveness."

2. Theological Preaching: "It's About God, Not You"

1. Elizabeth Sneed, "Dying for a Happy Ending," *USA Today*.

2. *Peculiar Speech* (Grand Rapids: William B. Eerdmans, 1992), 92-93.

3. I don't want to be misunderstood here. A great preacher who has influenced me is Theodore P. Ferris, who was a nervous wreck before he preached. The fearless Christian preacher may very well tremble when climbing into the pulpit; indeed, I cannot imagine a preacher *not* trembling when faced with this supreme responsibility. But this is the fear of God, properly understood, not the fear of human beings.

4. *Pastor* (Nashville: Abingdon, 2002).

5. *The Last Word* (Nashville: Abingdon, 2000), 16.

6. Christopher Lo Morse, *Not Every Spirit: A Dogmatics of Faithful Disbelief* (Valley Forge, Pa.: Trinity Press International, 1994).

7. Martin H. Copenhaver, Anthony B. Robinson, William H. Willimon, *Good News in Exile* (Grand Rapids: William B. Eerdmans, 1999), 52. In September 2003, as I was preparing this essay, the *Wall Street Journal* ran a review of a new book, *The Transformation of American Religion: How We Actually Live our Faith*, by Alan Wolfe. The caption reads, "In contemporary America, faith has met culture, and *culture has won*" (emphasis added).

8. Unpublished sermon, "Christian Leadership 101," Duke Chapel, August 26, 2001.

9. *Where Resident Aliens Live* (Nashville: Abingdon, 1996), 48. Emphasis added.

10. Charles L. Bartow, *God's Human Speech: A Practical Theology of Proclamation* (Grand Rapids: William B. Eerdmans, 1997). Emphasis added.

11. Ibid., 56n.

12. All quotations in this paragraph are from Willimon's chapter "Suddenly a Light from Heaven" in *Conversion in the Wesleyan Tradition*, edited by Kenneth J. Collins and John H. Tyson (Nashville: Abingdon, 2001).

13. Richard Hays, *The Faith of Jesus Christ: An Investigation of the Narrative Substructure of Galatians 3:1–4:11* (Chico, Calif.: Scholars Press, 1983). This celebrated article has been widely anthologized and disseminated.

14. *Good News in Exile*, 57.

15. *Peculiar Speech*, 80. Writing this essay has driven me back to Paul Holmer's *The Grammar of Faith* (San Francisco: Harper & Row, 1978), for which I am very grateful.

16. The possible exception would be Robert Farrar Capon, but although much of his work is genuinely valuable and biblical in the best sense, it is marred in my judgment by an excess of recklessness (to be distinguished from fearlessness) and an extreme antinomianism verging on irresponsibility—therefore not truly radical in the Pauline sense.

17. *Good News in Exile*, 45.

18. *Where Resident Aliens Live*, 59.

19. *Conversion in the Wesleyan Tradition*, 246. Emphasis added.

20. *Peculiar Speech*, 76.

21. *Pastor*, 213.

22. Ibid., 266.

23. *Conversion in the Wesleyan Tradition*, 249-50.

24. *Indirection* means launching into a story without cueing the reader. Example: "She was distraught when she walked into my office . . ." instead of "A distraught young woman walked into my office. . . ." Indirection was famously forbidden at the *New Yorker* magazine for forty years. It is common now, but still undesirable in many cases.

25. *Pastor*, 251.

26. Doutlas Harink, *Paul Among the Postliberals* (Grand Rapids: Brazos Press, 2003), 234.

3. Resident Aliens: "Christianity Is Weird, Odd, Peculiar"

1. See this volume, p. 56.

2. See this volume, p. 54.

3. See this volume, p. 55.

4. *Pastor: The Theology and Practice of Ordained Ministry* (Nashville: Abingdon, 2002), 253.

5. Ibid., 255.

6. Ibid.

7. Ibid., 257.

8. See this volume, p. 48.

9. "Suddenly a Light from Heaven," in Kenneth J. Collins and John H. Tyson, eds., *Conversion in the Wesleyan Tradition* (Nashville: Abingdon, 2001), 244.

10. Ibid., 249.

11. Ibid., 250.

4. Discipleship: "I Can't Believe You People Actually Want to Be Christians"

1. William H. Willimon, *The Intrusive Word: Preaching to the Unbaptized* (Grand Rapids: William B. Eerdmans, 1994), 5.

2. William H. Willimon, *Peculiar Speech: Preaching to the Baptized* (Grand Rapids: William B. Eerdmans, 1992), 32.

3. William H. Willimon, "Spin City Jesus" (in this volume, pp.78-79), preached at Duke University Chapel, September 9, 2001.

4. Ibid., 80.

5. Stanley Hauerwas and William H. Willimon, *Where Resident Aliens Live: Exercises for Christian Practice* (Nashville: Abingdon, 1996), 50.

6. Willimon, "Spin City Jesus," 79.

7. Ibid., 76.

8. R. E. C. Browne, *The Ministry of the Word* (Philadelphia: Fortress, 1976), 40.

9. Fred B. Craddock, *As One Without Authority*, as quoted in William H. Willimon, *Peculiar Speech*, 48.

10. Willimon, *Peculiar Speech*, 48-49.

11. Martin B. Copenhaver, Anthony B. Robinson, and Wiliam H. Willimon, *Good News in Exile: Three Pastors Offer a Hopeful Vision for the Church* (Grand Rapids: William B. Eerdmans, 1999), 55-56.

12. William H. Willimon, "Christianity: Following Jesus" (in this volume, p. 72), preached at Duke University Chapel, October 22, 2000.

13. Hauerwas and Willimon, *Where Resident Aliens Live*, 64-65.

14. William H. Willimon, "Summons to Ministry," *Christian Century* 118, no. 6 (February 21, 2001): 7.

15. Ibid.

16. Stanley Hauerwas as quoted in William H. Willimon, "Under Fire," *The Christian Century*, 118, no. 14 (May 2, 2001): 6.

5. Conversion and Transformation: "Christians Are Made, Not Born"

1. Anne Braden, *The Wall Between*, 27-28.

2. William H. Willimon, *Peculiar Speech: Preaching to the Baptized* (Grand Rapids: William B. Eerdmans, 1992), 82-86.

3. This is the subtitle of William H. Willimon's chapter, "Preaching and Speech," in *Good News in Exile: Three Pastors Offer a Hopeful Vision for the Church*, written together with Martin B. Copenhaver and Anthony B. Robinson (Grand Rapids: William B. Eerdmans, 1999), 45-57.

4. Willimon, *Peculiar Speech*, 87-88.

5. See chapter 10, "The Pastor as Prophet: Truth Telling in the Name of Jesus," in William H. Willimon, *Pastor: The Theology and Practice of Ordained Ministry* (Nashville: Abingdon, 2002), 249-65. See particularly his discussion of #4, *"The purpose of prophetic preaching is the production and equipment of a community of prophets."*

6. William H. Willimon, "Suddenly a Light from Heaven," in Kenneth J. Collins and John H. Tyson, eds., *Conversion in the Wesleyan Tradition* (Nashville: Abingdon, 2001), 248.

7. Ibid., 249.

8. See this volume, p. 9.

9. Willimon, "Suddenly a Light from Heaven," in *Conversion*, 243-44.

10. Ibid., 244-45.

11. William H. Willimon, "Fishing with Jesus," sermon preached at Duke University Chapel on January 24, 1999.

12. Willimon, "Preaching and Speech: Words Make Worlds," *Good News in Exile*, 55.

13. Willimon, "Suddenly a Light from Heaven," in *Conversion*, 241-42.

14. See, for example, William H. Willimon, *The Service of God: How Worship and Ethics Are Related* (Nashville: Abingdon, 1983).

15. Willimon, *Pastor: The Theology and Practice of Ordained Ministry*, 252.

16. See chapter 3, "Church and World," in Stanley Hauerwas and William H. Willimon, *Where Resident Aliens Live: Exercises for Christian Practice* (Nashville: Abingdon, 1996), 46-50.

17. Ibid., 64.

6. Explaining Why Will Willimon Never Explains

1. For my understanding of these matters as "metaphysical," see my chapter "Connections Created and Contingent: Aquinas, Preller, Wittgenstein, and Hopkins" in *Performing the Faith: Bonhoeffer and The Practice of Nonviolence* (Grand Rapids: Brazos Press, forthcoming).

2. The sermons "More" and "Here" can be found in our book *Preaching to Strangers* (Louisville: Westminster / John Knox Press, 1992), 113-34.

3. For Barth's most extensive discussion of sin, see *Church Dogmatics* 4/1, translated by G. W. Bromiley (New York: Scribner's Sons, 1956), 157-513.

4. See my "Introduction" to *Preaching to Strangers*, 1-15.

5. Stanley Hauerwas, *With the Grain of the Universe: The Church's Witness and Natural Theology* (Grand Rapids: Brazos Press, 2001), 173-84.

6. In his *The Spirit of Early Christian Thought* (New Haven: Yale University Press, 2003), Robert Wilken observes that when Augustine wrote about the Trinity he was not seeking "a theological concept or an explanation as such, but

the living God who is Father, Son, and Holy Spirit, the 'Trinity that is God, the true and supreme and only God,'" 108.

7. One place where the story of Gladys is told is in our *Resident Aliens: Life in the Christian Colony* (Nashville: Abingdon, 1989), 118-19.

8. Robert Wilken observes, "The Scriptures are the 'ground and pillar of our faith,' says Irenaeus. If the Bible is dismembered to serve an exotic theological program and biblical texts are deployed willy-nilly (as the Gnostics did), the Scriptures will remain a closed book and it will not be possible 'to find the truth in them.' Without a grasp of the plot that holds everything together, the Bible is as vacuous as a mosaic in which the tiles have been arbitrarily rearranged without reference to the original design or as a poem constructed by stringing together random verses from the *Iliad* and *Odyssey* and imagining it was Homer. . . . Whether one reads Athanasius against Arius, Augustine against Pelagius, or Cyril of Alexandria against Nestorius, all assume that individual passages are to be read in the light of the story that gives meaning to the whole." *The Spirit of Early Christian Thought*, 67-68.

7. It's Peculiar to Be a Prophet

1. Karl Barth, *Church Dogmatics* 3, 4.

2. Brueggemann's definition is found in his *Reverberations of Faith: A Theological Handbook of Old Testament Themes* (Louisville: Westminster / John Knox Press, 2002), 159-62.

Index of Names